The Dance

A Story of Love, Faith, and Survival

JOAN AUBELE

What people are saying about *The Dance*:

"The Dance touched my heart with its message to love, pray, and hang on in spite of difficult challenges. Joan's account of her battle with Stage 4 cancer mightily demonstrates where there is life, there is hope. Read it; you'll be blessed. I was."
- *Diana Zielinski*

"I am speechless. Tear ridden and speechless. The book is magnificent, meaningful, and more than inspiring. To think I spent the morning lamenting my knees are hurting, the lump in my jaw is growing, my kidneys are failing... well, you understand... quit complaining and move on to do the things God wants us to do - for others." - *Mary Ellen Aschenbrenner*

"I read *The Dance* non-stop. In fact, I couldn't put it down! This is by far the best written story I've read lately. This is an amazing work, with an amazing story. Your words are an inspiration, and I am now committed to walking every day, it is so important for my physical and spiritual health."
- *Shellie Dunn*

"I actually read your book at the hospital during my husband's surgery. It kept me interested in reading and not worrying. Thank you." - *Kim Boczko*

"Your memoir was so touching and moving, it brought tears to my eyes....This is a heartfelt, funny, REAL, not-at-all-sappy, insightful, moving book. I have, thankfully, never had cancer, but I felt what it was like to live through something like that, and to come out on the other end. It is as much about life and living as it is about illness and the fear of dying."
- *Julie Harte, Director of Somonauk Public Library*

JOAN AUBELE

The Dance

A Story of Love, Faith, and Survival

Joan Aubele

JOAN AUBELE

The Dance
A Story of Love, Faith, and Survival
By Joan Aubele
PO Box 653 Somonauk, Illinois 60552
Copyright © 2015 by Joan Aubele

I have tried to recreate events, locales and conversations from my memories of them. Some names and identifying details have been changed to protect the privacy of individuals. Every effort has been made to make this memoir as complete and as accurate as possible. However, there may be mistakes, both typographical and in content.

Edited by Stephen J. Dunn
Cover artwork Copyright © 2015 by Carl E. Aubele and Joan Aubele
Cover design by Joan Aubele and Sandy Champion
Book design and production by Joan Aubele and Stephen J. Dunn
Author photograph by élan studios
Quotation from the hymn, "Lord of the Dance," by Sydney Carter © 1963 Stainer & Bell, Ltd. (Admin. Hope Publishing Company, Carol Stream, IL 60188). All rights reserved. Used by permission.
Composed in Palatino Linotype

Published in the United States of America
First Edition, June 2015
10 9 8 7 6 5 4 3 2 1

Library of Congress Control Number: 2015908111
ISBN-13: 978-0692451328
ISBN-10: 0692451323

To my wonderful husband Carl. If not for your unwavering love of over thirty-seven years, your strength and never-ending support, I would not have been able to write this book. I thank God for bringing you into my life. You remind me of all the things I can do, instead of the things I cannot. Most importantly, thank you for always keeping me on my intended path.

JOAN AUBELE

~Forward~

I met Joanie on a Monday afternoon at a meeting of the Somonauk Library Writers Group. An attractive woman with a speech impediment started to speak, and her words went right to my heart. As the weeks went on, the more I heard, the more I realized her story was a diamond in the rough. All it needed was some editing by a pair of fresh eyes to make it sparkle.

Joanie and I recognized early on that we were kindred spirits. I am a paraplegic due to a spinal cord disease, and must use a wheelchair. We share many of the same medical, financial, and emotional experiences. I recently finished four months of chemo and radiation therapy for lymphoma. Being absorbed in Joanie's story took me out of myself.

Joanie is a talented lady. In addition to writing, and her inspirational work, she makes colorful designer scarves as vibrant as her personality.

This story is important because at that time, Joanie was the only adult survivor of the "childhood" cancer. Her journey is unique, as every cancer patient's journey is unique. Yet her story is repeated millions upon millions of times a day all around the globe.

Although I am not a person of faith, as Joanie is, I believe in her. And that is sufficient to the day.

Stephen Dunn
May 2015

JOAN AUBELE

~A Note From the Author~

The story you are about to embark upon is entirely true. Events have not been modified or changed to add dramatic flair. Exaggerations were not needed.

I am neither a sports superstar, nor a Hollywood actor. I haven't set any world records, nor have I won the Nobel Peace Prize. I am simply an ordinary woman who has lived an extraordinary life filled with many miracles which need to be shared. This inspirational memoir has been written with the sole intention of stressing the importance of living one's life to the fullest - to appreciate everything around you, and to live for one another each and every day!

JOAN AUBELE

~Table of Contents~

JOAN AUBELE

Let them praise His name with dancing; Let them sing praises to Him with timbrel and lyre. For the LORD takes pleasure in His people; He will beautify the afflicted ones with salvation.

Psalm 149:3-4

JOAN AUBELE

This now makes complete sense. Leukemia is a cancer of the blood-forming tissue throughout the entire body; ergo - *head to toe*.

Some may think I'm in-tune with my body, or that I have a super keen sense of intuition, but I believe it's the Holy Spirit.

Now, before you discount me as a woman who when faced with a life-threatening illness, has "found God," hear me out.

The deep connection I feel with the Lord began when I was eight years old, when I received my First Holy Communion. Each time I receive this sacrament, love permeates my soul. I choke back tears I feel His presence so deeply. Current problems of the week disappear, and are replaced with a sense of calm.

The first time I experienced this real closeness was when I was seventeen. I was helping my mom get ready for my baby sister's birthday party. As I set the table with serving trays and dishes, it hit me.

I'm pregnant! I thought.

No, I'm not claiming this is another Immaculate Conception. I was just a naive high school senior who didn't even *think* about pregnancy, let alone during the party preparations.

Okay, think this through. First I have to tell Carl, and then we need to visit an OB, I rationalized.

I didn't know the first thing about pregnancy, but did hear somewhere that pregnant women need special vitamins. *I'll have to get some of those*, I told myself quite adult-like.

I began to panic, random thoughts popped into my head.

Oh God, Mom's gonna kill me!
How and why do I know I'm PG?

*Oh, and Dad's **really** gonna kill me!*
Breathe… it'll be okay.

I first noticed Carl in my high school Spanish class, freshman year, 1974, but his good looks and swollen muscles scared me away. His long, wavy, dark brown hair fell across his broad shoulders as he flashed me a boyish grin. My mother warned me about boys like him. She never explained why, just that I should be careful – so I heeded her confusing advice - until my junior year of high school anyway.

I was dating a boy, named Bill, off and on, but also had my eyes on Danny. Danny was also dating someone else off and on, but had his eye on me as well. Danny and I were loyal to our significant others and never seemed to be "available" at the same time (your typical high school drama).

Danny asked a buddy to date me to keep me occupied during one of my 'off' times with Bill. Danny's intention was to "move in" when he broke up with his girlfriend. Danny's plan backfired. That buddy was Carl and we soon fell in love.

Since I was seventeen, I required written permission from my parents to wed. Plan A was to marry with our families' blessings, but if we had to resort to plan B, we would. Plan B was to move out-of-state down south where it was legal to marry at sixteen. I hoped for plan A.

A few weeks passed before we led my dad into a room downstairs, telling him that we needed to talk to him about something important in private.

"Dad, I'm pregnant," I shook. "Carl and I want to get married, but I need your permission."

I held my breath. Even though it was a few moments, it felt like hours. He gazed silently at us, as we awaited the dreaded response.

"You should wait until *after* the baby is born. You can live in the basement for now," he finally said. "Once the baby is born, see if you still want to get married. Couples that marry for the wrong reason, only end up divorced."

His pronouncement sounded certain and final.

"But Dad, we're not getting married because we're pregnant, it's because we're in love. We planned to get married and have children someday *anyway*," I trembled. "There's no reason to wait. We *are* following our original plan; just not in the order we expected."

Since it was obvious we had made up our minds, Dad was skeptical, but gave us his blessing. It would be Plan A, after all.

It was, however, important to me that we marry in the Catholic Church. This required at least six months of matrimonial preparation classes, but we didn't have that much time. We wanted to be married *before* the baby was born.

The parish we attended directed us to Catholic Charities to see if they could somehow speed up the process. Carl pumped gas after school and on the weekends, so our financial future didn't look very promising.

"We cannot sanction your marriage," the counselor concluded. "The odds are stacked against you. You're very young to marry in the first place, let alone adding a baby into the mix. You haven't even finished high school."

I can't blame them. They thought, like so many, that we were two teenagers who *think* they are in love - infatuation being confused with love. The reality of a hard life ahead would most likely end in divorce. Everyone thought we were doomed to fail.

We left their office and telephoned our priest friend from Chicago to request his help. He contacted Catholic Charities, pleaded our case once again, pulled a few strings, and we were permitted to make our sacred vows. Despite his residence in the Chicago diocese, he was even allowed to preside over the ceremony in our hometown church in Woodridge. We managed to pull off that church wedding in a few short months.

We didn't have two nickels to rub together, as my grandfather used to say, but we were over-the-moon giddy.

Our studio, garden apartment was decorated lavishly. A Jimmy Hendrix poster hung on the living room wall. Mismatched, donated furniture sparsely filled the space. Carl made shelves out of wood boards and cinder blocks, placing hub-caps on either end. Large, black globe lights fastened by gold chains hung from the ceiling. The typewriter stand we garbage picked served as a kitchen table.

A homemade, wooden bassinet was lent to us by my uncle. Unable to afford a bed for two, we pushed our twin mattresses from my parents' home together, holding them in place with a foam insert. Each morning we would laugh at who "fell in the crack" before we pushed them back together again.

Carl's brother Rich felt sorry for us because we didn't have a TV, so he gave us one. We'd sit on the floor, almost on top of it, to view the nine-inch screen. "Hey, where'd the binoculars go, it's my turn!" we'd joke.

One time, a friend stopped by the apartment with my favorite – chocolate cream pie. A dishwasher at *Poppin' Fresh Pies* restaurant, he mysteriously ended up with one of these in his possession by the end of his shift.

Mom was impressed when Carl and I bought matching gym shoes one month.

"You guys must be doing pretty well," mom commented.

Yup, we were living large!

JOAN AUBELE

We never know what tomorrow will bring, or what curve ball might be thrown our way, so he needs to get some rest.

We never say "good-bye," for fear it may be the last time, so we are careful to say, "Good-night."

Dr. M pulls Carl aside in the hallway. "Her death is inevitable; you need to discuss funeral arrangements."

"Do you…have a burial spot you prefer?" Carl whispers in my ear.

"It doesn't matter *where* I'm buried. Choose whatever cemetery is most convenient for you and the girls," I swallow.

I begin to choose the hymns I want played at my funeral.

All of a sudden, Carl announces, "Wait a minute…we can't just give up!"

We decide to stop accepting my death so permissibly. I feel a sudden surge of determination to fight the fight of my life, or at least go out swinging.

"You're right. I'm gonna fight like hell. I am *not* going to leave our babies without a mother!" I say through the sobs.

My oncologist, Dr. Madhavan, is a woman of East Indian decent. Her accent apparent, she speaks in a clear and precise manner. She has an olive complexion and wears her long, thick, black hair pulled neat into a pony tail. She always wears a kind smile for me. Even though she is my senior by fourteen years, she somehow reminds me of my mother. She is gentle with me, but she has a no-nonsense approach with her co-workers. She is good at what she does, and expects no less from others.

She is diligent in her detailed explanation of the three phases of chemotherapy treatment.

"The first part is called induction, the second - consolidation, and the third - maintenance," she explains. "This will involve a combination of drugs. The induction phase will bring you into remission. Next, is the consolidation portion, a more intense therapy that will sustain your remission. And then, maintenance. This chemotherapy will be given in lower doses on an out-patient basis to assist in prolonging your remission."

A surgeon inserts a VAP (venous access port) into my chest for admission of chemotherapy, medications, and much needed blood supplies. A central venous catheter is a tube that goes into a vein in your chest and ends at your heart. It is then attached to the VAP by another tube which now dangles from my chest. It's also used to take the numerous blood draws I'll need to monitor my progress.

The induction chemotherapy begins four days after I'm admitted. Carl later tells me the reason for the delay was that my cancer was so advanced, they didn't think I would live till the end of the week, so why put me through dreadful chemotherapy?

If I'm not crying, I am praying, usually both. Father Bob, a sandy-brown haired man with dark glasses that frame his clean-shaven, chiseled face is the hospital Chaplain. He is tall and thin. But then again, everyone looks tall when you are lying flat in a bed. Father Bob and I speak about life, and about death.

"Think of your struggles as a roller coaster ride; it has its many ups and downs, you need to hold on tight for the ride!" he says.

On the days I'm not too weak or vomiting, Father Bob brings the Sacrament of Holy Communion to me. As he places the Host upon my tongue, I imagine Jesus Christ sharing it with me.

I do the same when Father Bob places his hand on my forehead to bless me. I picture the Lord healing me with his loving touch. Father Bob performs the Anointing of the Sick sacrament – the first of many. I sob as I feel God's presence.

Several months prior to my diagnosis, every time I tilted my head back to rinse my hair in the shower, shooting pains jabbed in my skull. I began to think my severe pain was brain related. I shared my revelation with Carl and he thought I was nuts. But I was the one at home all day. Carl was at work, and Theresa and Allison were away at school. Natalie didn't appear to suffer from these horrific headaches. We had the gas company come out and check the pipes for leaks anyway.

No leaks. It was just me.

When I first experienced those monster headaches, I confided in a woman named Debbie Q. We had become casual friends through our Aurora babysitting exchange. She survived a brain aneurism and I had a lot of questions for her.

My current diagnosis of cancer prompts me to write Debbie Q a long letter. Death had knocked at her door as a young mother as well. We must share a lot of similar feelings.

She generously responds with silk flower arrangements, and a card a week with letters of encouragement tucked inside. I look forward to those letters. I hang onto every word.

As I lay in my hospital bed, I yearn for the mother I once had as a little girl, to be protected, a feeling only a mother can give. If she could control her illness she would be here for me. But I know she can't, any more than I can with mine.

My mother was diagnosed a manic-depressive and paranoid schizophrenic when I was fourteen. She attempted suicide numerous times throughout my high school years, which left her exhausted and mentally debilitated.

We lived in a Chicago two-flat for most of my childhood, her mother and father, my grandparents, lived downstairs. She chased after five children, tended to the basement wringer washing machine, starched and pressed wardrobes for seven, and prepared a delicious dessert for after every dinner. I don't know how Mom did it, but she managed to make two visits a day to grandma's downstairs as well.

Our social calls consisted of Grandma's ice tea and *Salerno* butter cookies. We placed the cookies on our fingers and pretended they were glamorous rings. Sometimes Grandma would treat us to root beer flavored *Shasta* pop or an ice-cream bar from Pete's Grocery on the corner.

We moved to west suburban Woodridge, and Grandma passed away just a few months later. Mom had always been a stay-at-home mother, but now took a part-time job at JC Penny. There were just too many major changes in her life at once. The uprooting from a Chicago lifestyle, the new job, and the death of her mother caused a nervous breakdown.

Mom sunk deeper and deeper into depression, her grip on reality growing ever more tenuous. The mentally ill were not treated the way they should be, and she was put on many different medications. This only seemed to make her worse.

It would have been easier to accept her behavior if she stared out the window. But every once in a while I got a glimmer of hope and the return of the mom I once knew, before she slipped away again. I kept my emotions and troubles from Mom because I never knew how she'd react. I feared, as all my sisters, that we would be the one who would trigger the successful suicide.

My thoughts drift back to my favorite childhood holiday - Christmas. My mother's brothers and sister take turns hosting our annual Christmas Eve party. Grandma and Grandpa, aunts and uncles, with the many cousins, gather in one of my aunts' basements (the only space large enough to accommodate forty plus people).

A million different types of cookies are spread out on one of many tables. Salads, hors d'oeurves, veggie trays, meats, and, of course, the mandatory Jell-o mold are displayed as well.

We balance plates on our laps, careful not to spill on our new Christmas outfits. Mom dresses us in coordinated flocks, and places a velvet bow in our hair for this joyous occasion. We look simply adorable.

Uncle Gene plays the guitar as he leads us in song.

"If you sing real loud, maybe Santa will hear us and come down our chimney," he suggests.

We sing our hearts out, and lo and behold – Santa arrives!

Aunt Marge delightedly uses her movie camera to document the festivities.

On the car ride home, Dad finds the radio station broadcasting that Santa's sleigh has been spotted in the sky above our town.

"Quick, look out the window. I think I see Rudolph's red nose," Mom says with excitement.

"I think I see him!" my sister Terrie calls out.

"Me too!" Ellie squeals.

"All girls and boys are to go to bed as quickly as possible, so Santa can come to your house to deliver presents," the radio announcer cautions.

We fall asleep on the long car ride home, and Dad carries us upstairs one by one. I don't know if my sisters are faking it, like I am, but I love being held close and safely tucked into bed.

I now wish that my biggest problem is not to get home before Santa arrives.

Twenty-five units of blood, eighty-two platelet transfusions, and four units of fresh-frozen blood are required to keep me alive.

Sudden massive blood inputs cause horrible headaches, and provoke me to chastise the Infectious Disease Specialist to use a whisper upon his entry. Even the sounds of my own breathing hurt.

A morphine pump is hooked up for the debilitating headaches.

"Don't be afraid to squeeze the button as often as necessary. You won't overdose, I promise. It's already set for the allotted amount," hushes a nurse.

I squeeze and squeeze that button. For the first and only time, I ask a nurse to tell Carl not to come today.

A few days later, Carl discovers a huge lump on the side of my neck, which is painful to the touch. He notifies a nurse, and within the few minutes it takes her to come into my room, the lump doubles in size.

Emergency surgery is performed to remove a fungus that has lodged in my jugular. The blood that pumps from my brain to my heart is blocked, and is pooling in the vital vein. Ultrasound also detects fungi around my heart and lungs, which need to be dissolved with medication.

I'm unaware of this at the time, but the surgeon suggests Carl contact family to say their good-byes. I most likely won't make it through surgery.

It's expected that this will be a forty-five minute procedure, but it turns into a three hour ordeal.

Against all odds, I miraculously survive the life-threatening surgery.

"You still need to be prepared for her death," the surgeon says. "She may not make it through the night."

Father Bob performs the Anointing of The Sick once again.

By this time, entire church congregations pray for the young mother of three who is fighting for her life. I know of at least nine who are.

After several hours, Carl calls my father's home to reach my sister Donna at the other end. Carl asks, "Where the hell is everyone?"

"Dad said you didn't want us to come," she replies.

My sisters must have gathered at Dad's house, to wait for the call informing them of my death.

I think it's cool that my sisters happen to come to see me **at the very same time**. (I told you I was naive.) Sadly, my father never comes.

The next morning, Dr. M and several nurses are thrilled as they enter my room to congratulate me. I think it is at this point I begin to believe that miracles still occur.

I manage to skate by, and the fungus around my heart and lungs disappears.

I look forward to Thursdays when Carl brings the three girls to the hospital to see me. No matter how terrible I feel, or how exhausted I am, I sit up in bed and smile as their bright eyes peep over their little, masked faces. I listen to stories filled with excitement about their school week. They bring in drawings and cards which always make me cry. I remind Theresa and Allison, as I cry tears of joy, how happy Mommy is to see their beautiful artwork.

Carl places Natalie on my bed, but I am too weak to hold her on my own. I also fear she'll pull out one of the many cords dangling from my body. Carl holds her for me. My visits with the girls aren't very long, fatigue soon overwhelms me.

"I've set the bunk-beds up in Allison and Natalie's room. Mom's gonna stay at the house for a bit, until you come home," Carl informs. "This way the girls can share a room, so Mom has her own. See, it'll all work out, now you just concentrate on getting better!" he smiles.

When I awake one morning, everything looks fuzzy. I must have lost a contact during the night. Beverly, one of the nurses, crawls on her hands and knees to search for it, but never finds it. They warn that I shouldn't wear them anyway.

My glasses are broken and at home, so Carl explains the situation to the eye doc. I am given a new pair, but they are God awful big! Like 1970 big.

Blind without them, I can't seem to hear anyone if I can't see their faces. So now whenever Dr. M comes into my room, I have her wait until I put my glasses on before she speaks. She now refers to them as my "thinking glasses."

One of my ports becomes infected, removed, and another surgery replaces it with a new one. This happens twice. The infection site is cleansed several times a day. I won't pretend to tell you I know what is being done to me, for I need to look away. The thought of what they are doing makes me nauseous.

The process involves a saline solution to flush the infected site. "We have to irrigate the wound," is how they explain it to me. It feels cool at first, then hurts like hell. Once again I depend on my Lamaze breathing. Who knew I'd be using *that* so often?

Since I no longer have an immune system, I require a private room because my environment needs to be germ free. When anyone enters, they are instructed to scrub their hands, and put on a gown and mask. I am not permitted to have fresh flowers and plants due to mold, so I am surrounded with artificial ones. I cannot eat fresh fruits or vegetables, and yogurt is taken off my menu.

"You shouldn't even kiss Carl," warns a nurse.

Seriously?

JOAN AUBELE

~Chapter Three~

When I first arrived at Mercy Hospital, snow covered the ground. The world has moved forward without me. Spring is here. I know this because as I lie in bed and gaze out the window, I can see the snow has melted, and warm rays of sunshine dance across my bed.

Early one April morning, Carl holds the hand of what appears to be a little angel. Allison stands beside my bed. Her dark blonde hair is tucked beneath a veil. Freckles sprinkle her nose. She grins up at me. Her innocent smile, minus a few front teeth, melts my heart.

She beams enthusiastically, and proudly shows off her beautiful, white, First Holy Communion dress, adorned with lace and silk. She spins as she models the dress her grandmother has made. A shiny gold cross dangles from a necklace around her neck. I force a smile, as I mask the sadness which washes over me. I'm reminded not only did I miss out on *this* special day, but I may miss out on her entire life.

Both Carl and Alice, my mother-in-law, agree of the importance to maintain some sort of normalcy in the girls' lives. A party in Allison's honor is planned for later in the day. While standing at the grill, Carl's brother, John, asks him if there is anything he can do. (He means with me being in the hospital.) But Carl replies, "Flip the burgers." That's one of the many things I admire about Carl - his ability to stay focused, to live in the now, and not worry about what the uncertain future may bring. Take each problem as it comes. Simply *"flip the burgers."*

Late one night - actually closer to morning - I'm freaking out. Aware of the time, I hesitate to call Carl and wake him, but I can't help it, I dial anyway.

"What will happen to the girls if I leave them motherless?" I shriek into the phone. "Will they ever truly recover? Will they think I've abandoned them? And what about you, how will you ever manage to raise three girls on your own?"

"You're getting ahead of yourself," Carl reassures. "Let's take it one day at a time," he says as if he has a plan. "The girls will be fine, and besides, you're not going anywhere!"

We speak till dawn before he calms me down enough to fall back asleep.

I have several compassionate phone conversations with my sister, Terrie, in Georgia. I'm fourteen months older, but we looked a lot alike when we were children. We took delight when people smiled and asked if we were twins. Mom added to the confusion by dressing us identically. We laugh and we cry as we reminisce about our childhood and the trouble we got into as teenagers. We try to stay positive. We talk about growing old and sharing a place together. We joke and poke fun at one another.

"You'll see. Someday we'll be sitting in rocking chairs on our front porch, comparing our aches and pains," Terrie says.

"You young whippersnappers - get off my lawn," I play along.

I am comforted by the foolishness. We pretend as though things are normal, at least for a little while.

My sisters take turns staying at the house with the girls. Pregnant sister, Terrie, drives up from Georgia to stay for a week.

Since so many people are coming in and out of the house, and no one knows where things are, Terrie, intending to make it easier on everyone, labels each kitchen cabinet. One is marked 'silverware', another 'utensils', 'pots and pans', 'plates', 'cups', etc.

Carl comes home from work, and rips the labels off. "She's not dead yet!" he growls, and marches into the bedroom, slamming the door behind him.

Terrie understands that emotions are high; none of us has ever had to deal with anything like this before.

Terrie brings with her an inspirational "Footprints" plaque. Carl presents it to me in the hospital. I begin to sob.

I cry a lot these days. I am overwhelmed. Despite the strong possibility I may die, and leave my children motherless, I am, at the same time, grateful for the kindness of others. They have put their own lives on hold to help me and Carl. I think most of my tears, though, are from the love I feel from the Lord.

It's almost 4:00 - enough time before Carl comes to visit. A commode sits a few feet from the bed. Usually I'm too weak to walk to the bathroom, but I feel strong today, and I decide to touch myself up a little. I do myself proud as I wobble past the commode, dragging the IV tree, and go the distance to the bathroom. Ah, success!

But when I look in the mirror, I'm horrified! Is this monster staring back at me what Carl has gawked at each day?

But the Infectious Disease guy said I had a beautiful head. He said I looked like a rock star! He lied.

Upon Carl's arrival, I confess my appearance embarrasses me, and I want to hide.

"I've watched this happen gradually. I don't even see it anymore," he replies as he hugs my scrawny body. "You're seeing yourself for the first time, that's all."

"By the way," Carl says, "your sisters mentioned that their husbands want to stop by."

"I don't want any of the brothers-in-law coming to visit. I look terrible."

"But they want to see you," Carl replies.

"Sorry, I just can't."

My thoughts sound vain in my ears. Shame on me for caring what I look like. With all that I face, hair loss should be the least of my worries. But I grieve for the Joan that has disappeared.

I haven't been permitted to leave my room other than for the occasional CT scan, ultrasound, or MRI. Today is different.

"How would you like to go for a short cruise outside?" a nurse burst with enthusiasm. "Dr. Madhavan said it's okay."

Without hesitation, I slide into a wheelchair and don the required mask. The nurse snugly wraps me in blankets like a cocoon. We flee down the hallway to the solarium. It overlooks the entire facility. I see women enter and exit Dr. Zapata's office across the street. They all seem happy. The good news after their check-ups shows on their faces. They are not being sent to the ER like I was. I enjoy people-watching and notice everyone rush around. The world continues to turn despite my standing still.

We head for the elevators, and go for our full-fledged escape. The elevator moves in slow motion, stopping at each floor. Floor three. People get off with bouquets of flowers before more people get in. At floor two the doors open again. *Hurry up* people!

We finally arrive on the first floor. We plunge out the sliding hospital doors into the grand sunshine. Its warmth penetrates the many blanket layers which feels divine. Tears spill over my mask as an immense gratitude consumes me. *Thank you Lord, for letting me still be a part of this world to see this magnificent day.*

The chemo's goal is to kill all the cancerous cells, but in doing so, also kills the good ones. The hope is to begin to produce new cells leading to remission.

I'm told to picture the Pac-Man video game with Pac-Man chomping on the bad cells. Banners of these goofy characters eating bad cells adorn my room.

Jo, a member from Alice's parish, St. Scholastica, is planning a pilgrimage to Medjugorje. Medjugorje was, and still is, an exceptional Holy place. Special intentions are collected and placed before the statue of the Blessed Mother asking that she present them to Christ her son.

"Anyone who wants an intention heard, write it down and I'll take it with me," offers Jo.

Alice writes her petition for my healing to Our Lady, places it in an envelope, and gives it to Jo.

Sometime later, a bone marrow aspiration is repeated. It discovers the amazing presence of white blood cells. Further blood tests show a sustained increase. The Lord has heard my nonstop prayers and has miraculously granted my healing.

I'm not so bold as to say the healing is of my doing, but rather maybe my desperate plea to let me live for my children's sake has been heard. Who knows? Maybe this is God's plan all along. I'll have to ask Him someday when I reach the Pearly Gates.

It has been documented that over two-hundred Marian apparitions have occurred since James the Elder in 40A.D. One particular visit was on June 24, 1981, when the "Queen of Peace" appeared before two sisters in Medjugorje, Bosnia. Though thousands of messages have been given since then, six are primary - conversion, prayer, fasting, faith, peace, and reconciliation.

"Pray as much as you can, pray however you can, but pray more always," says Our Lady.

"God wants to save you and sends you messages through men, nature, and so many things which can only help you to understand that you must change the direction of your life."

At long last, Carl and I are given the thumbs up to kiss again. I decide this is a momentous occasion requiring an official ceremony. I ask Carl to help me stand, and I dramatically shove my IV tree out of the way. We wrap trembling arms around one another. A chill pulses through my body as our lips meet. I close my eyes and sob as I relive our first teenage kiss.

After being hospitalized for almost six weeks, I am allowed to go home for Easter Sunday. I am anxious and frightened. Nights are the worst. My fevers reach their highest then, and with all the strange complications, I've become dependent on knowing a nurse is only the push of a button away. I want to go home, but I want to take Dr. Madhavan and all my nurses with me.

Nonsense. I'm over-reacting. I'm going home. Yay!

I shed joyful tears as Carl and I pull up the gravel driveway, and my heart leaps when I see my modest, thirty-three-year-old ranch house.

Carl carries my frail body as he reintroduces me to each room. We had just moved here to small-town Newark, Illinois three months ago, downsizing from our much larger, brand-new, two-story home in the Fox Valley Villages in Aurora. Carl's work hours had been cut big-time; and we could no longer afford to live there. I wanted the best of both worlds - to be a stay-at-home mom, but to live in a big house.

Even though I had agreed the move was necessary, I resented it. I'm embarrassed to admit I placed so much value on a stupid building. I let it overshadow what was truly important - my family.

Dumb! My priorities were lost. God saw fit to hit me over the head with a sledge-hammer to get the message across. Tragedy is quick to put everything into perspective.

Now I am grateful for the old closet doors that fall from their hinges, amused at the bedroom pocket-door which gets stuck, and no longer care about the scratched, raw, hardwood, living room floor. I couldn't care less if I had come home to a cardboard box. I am alive and I am home!

The nostalgic tour ends, and we sit outside on the old, front porch swing. I admire the beautiful surroundings. I am humbled by the simple things - the smell of fresh air, the vibrant shades of green of dancing grass and blooming flowers and sprouting trees. The birds entertain me as they sing love songs to each other. I gaze upon the robins as they hop around the front yard in search of juicy worms.

Tears trickle down my cheeks. The warm sun on my face reminds me I'm alive. Goosebumps surface as I'm suddenly aware of everything around me. It's breathtaking! These beautiful things have always been here, but I was too busy going through life's meaningless motions to pay attention to their beauty. I am grateful to experience all God's wonders.

Later that evening, Mercy Hospital phones to summon me to begin round two - the 'consolidation' portion of the treatment. My Easter weekend retreat is over.

Here we go again!

Alice has counted the collections at St. Scholastica's for years. One Monday morning she runs into Jo.

"I'm afraid to ask, but how's your daughter-in-law doing?" Jo asks.

"Much better, thanks. Her white blood cells have returned and are steadily climbing. She was even permitted to go home for Easter Sunday," Alice exclaims.

"I wonder ... do you remember which day this recovery began?" Jo questions.

"Thursday, April 12th. I remember this because I was readying for Mass on Holy Thursday when I got the call."

"That was the exact day I climbed Apparition Hill in Medjugorje and offered your petition," Jo says.

Jo and Alice hug in celebration. The Pastor, Father Thomas Sularz, overhears, and recommends it be documented in the church.

Specialists from all over the country call to discuss my status. As the sole adult survivor of Acute Lymphocytic Leukemia, they are interested to learn how the disease responds to treatment. Only one other woman had reached my stage. She has since died, so I am looked on as a lab rat.

But tests reveal cancer cells have reached my brain.

"We all have a brain barrier; a protection of sorts," Dr. Madhavan explains. "Chemo must therefore be increased twenty-fold to infiltrate the barrier."

This time the poison they choose is ARA-C. (Arabinosylcytosine) The nurses take turns to explain the chemical's potent side effects.

"You will have temporary symptoms similar to MS or Cerebral Palsy, in addition to all the side effects you've already experienced," says Carol.

I can't fathom it being any worse. I am so terribly weak already. The gut-wrenching vomiting and horrible diarrhea are unbearable. High fevers and peeling skin contribute to my pain. The metal taste in my mouth has made my appetite vanish. I force myself to drink the *Ensure* vitamin supplements the nurses insist upon.

"This will be even harder than before," adds Leah.

I'm terrified – but what is the alternative?

Daily visits from Carol and Leah develop into wonderful friendships. We talk about our kids, our husbands, our hopes and dreams, as we look to the future.

Leah is a bit younger than I, and we hit it off right away. Down to earth, she's easy to talk to. Her brown, curly, shoulder-length hair bounces as she rushes in and out of sight.

Carol sports a dark brown, shorter haircut, with slight waves that curl around her ears. I feel her warm smile each time she gently speaks.

I am comfortable confiding my innermost feelings with Carol. One day, as I hang onto her while she assists me to the commode, I break down. I can't put my emotions into words. "I feel so old, so defeated," I say. Carol knows how I feel and hugs me. "I understand," she empathizes.

I tell her something I've never said in my entire life. "I want to die! I can't take this any longer."

I quickly feel guilty for uttering these words. I'm embarrassed and ashamed. *How can I be so selfish? I don't really want to die, I just want this suffering to end.* Carol reminds me the feelings I have are my own, and I should never feel guilty for them.

I become depressed. One of the nurses calls Carl with her concern – my positive attitude is a must for recovery. The following day, Carl surprises me and brings all three girls to the hospital. He plops Natalie on the bed as if to say, "You're giving up on them?"

As I look into the eyes of these three beautiful children, I find the will to fight once again. Carl knows this is the boost I need.

His beautiful, green eyes twinkle each time he smiles. God, I love this man!

I can tell by Carl's big smile that he is ready to explode with some sort of news.

"My mom says yesterday the doorbell rang after she put Natalie down for her nap. Three extremely nervous women, stood in the doorway.

"'We're not sure what you're running here, but we pride ourselves in that Newark is a family community!' one said.

"'We've observed one young man, and several different women coming in and out of your house, but not leaving till the next morning,' another one chimed in.

"Mom said she began to laugh, Carl continues. His grin widens, he looks like the cat who swallowed the canary.

"'That's my son, and those women are his sisters!' Mom told them. 'His wife is in the hospital, and they are helping out with the children.'

"'Ohhhh,' they said in unison and quickly left."

They remind me of Gladys Kravitz on the "Bewitched" TV show, as she peaks through the curtains. "ABNER, come quick!" Only there's no magic to conceal, just a family's pathetic undoing.

I notice Carl has become quite thin, losing some of those swollen muscles he's had since high school. The stress is affecting him. He's being pulled in a million directions - my illness, caring for the girls, his job.

I'm rolled downstairs for one of my many tests. I am covered up to my chin in blankets, and wear a mask. My eyes alone are visible. Don, the orderly, who has delivered me many times before, makes an observation.

"You're eyes are so blue ... so beautiful," he pretends to flirt. His attempt to cheer me up is futile. Later that day, when Carl arrives, he comments on my eyes as well. But he says they are "freakishly crystal blue."

Don, the orderly, did not exaggerate, a nurse explains. It's yet another bizarre reaction to the potent chemo.

On May 6th, wedding goblets in hand, Carl cheerfully enters my room to celebrate our twelfth anniversary. His smile turns to shock as he watches me stare at the ceiling.

What's going on? No matter how hard I try, words won't come out. I scream inside. *Can't anyone hear me? Somebody help me!*

I can't move either! I don't understand what's going on! Maybe I've died, and don't know it.

Carl rushes and returns with a nurse. My wild eyes frantically beg for help. She talks to me - so I must still be alive.

The nurse asks, "Can you move *anything*?"

I lift my right index finger.

"Okay, good. I'll ask you yes or no questions. Lift your finger once if the answer means yes, and twice if the answer means no."

The nurses' guessing game is usually successful, but only after they have exhausted every possible question. "Am I in pain?" "Have I slipped down in bed and need adjustment?" "Do I need the bedpan?" I sometimes get confused as to which code means what.

Up once means yes, or does it mean no? Oh, I don't remember. I can't even recall what I wanted in the first place!

I answer "Yes" to the bedpan question even though that's not what I want. I would hate for her to waste a trip.

Next time I'll keep repeating to myself until she comes in.

A feeding tube is inserted up my nose and down my throat. The tape they use to secure it to my face itches, but I cannot move to scratch.

This is so darn uncomfortable. I feel the cold liquid as it passes through the tube. It's gross. If I could gag, I would.

On one of his rare visits, my father enters my room to find a zombie lying in my bed. A neurologist evaluates her. Dad glances at Carl, somberly slumped in a chair beside me.

He turns toward the serious man at my bedside, and demands, "What happened to her? Why? How long will she be like this?"

"It is a reaction to the chemotherapy," the doctor replies. "The human brain is so complex, there is no way to predict how long she'll be like this. It could be a day, or it could be a month. There's no way to tell."

Dad, disgusted and angered by his answers, stomps out of the room.

Carl follows him into the hallway. "I think we need to talk," he says.

"There is nothing to talk about!" Dad retorts, and storms away.

My left eye and side of my face begin to twitch. I pop up and lean over the side of the bed like something from *The Exorcist*.

Lord, now what is happening?

Someone places foam cushions around the bed rails so I won't injure myself. I yank the feeding tube out of my nose during a violent seizure. Despite my inner protests, the nurse tries twice to reinsert it. Dr. M is called in and she resituates the nasty tube.

Each time I convulse, Carl holds me down. "Please lie down, you'll hurt yourself!" he begs.

I have left my body and float above the bed. I peer down at a poor crazy woman wiggling like a fish out of water.

I cannot speak other than to utter, "I love you. I'm sorry."

"I love you. I'm sorry."

I must be dying, so I want to say it one last time.

"I'm sorry to put you through all of this - and for leaving you."

These are the last words I speak.

One evening, Orderly Don is instructed to weigh me. He rolls my unresponsive body from one side to the other, and slides a swing of some sort beneath me. I feel like a limp bag of bones. I'm hoisted like an animal to the slaughter.

The next day, someone is kind enough to turn the TV on for me. But, unable to speak, I stare blindly at a foggy screen for hours until Carl comes in and places my glasses upon my face.

You know the old saying, "for every door that is closed, God opens a window?" My ears become the windows, and my tether, to the world. I can't turn my head to look at the clock, so the rolling of the meal carts squeaking in the hallway gives me a good idea of the time throughout the day.

I remember how they come at around 6:00 a.m. to serve breakfast, again around noon for lunch, and at 6:00 p.m. for dinner. Since the feeding tube serves my nutritional needs, the meals are of no consequence. I have nowhere to go where I need to know the time, but something as simple as hearing that metal clunk in the halls, gives me some sense of connection.

Even though I'm unable to receive Communion at this time, Father Bob pops his head into the room and reminds me to "hold on tight." His presence is critical to me.

The diligent nurses roll me from side to side to prevent bedsores. My hands and feet peel from the chemo, so they slather them with lotion. My lips are dried out too, so ointment is applied. They swab the inside of my mouth to deter mouth sores.

Due to my bizarre complications, I require a twenty-four hour private duty nurse. All of them are wonderful, but Sandy is my favorite. She has bright blue eyes that shine with enthusiasm and compassion, a round, open face, and a brown, page-boy haircut.

Sandy leans in and repeatedly whispers into my ear, "Don't you give up on me! Don't you give up on your precious babies!"

Sandy chats through her routine of precise pillow placement under stress points. She speaks as if I will answer. "I'll place a pillow here, and place a pillow there." She grabs a pillow and says, "I'm going to put one in-between your ears." Realizing what she said, she bursts into laughter and apologizes profusely.

"I'm so sorry. I'm not laughing at you; I'm laughing at myself."

I think it's hilarious, but I have no way to let her know.

Aaron, a tall, slender, African-American man is my assigned physical therapist. He exercises my extremities to prevent atrophy. He methodically raises and bends my arms before attending to my legs, all the while speaking in a kind and gentle manner.

After a period of time, I am able to lift my legs on my own. I look forward to these sessions so much, whenever Aaron enters my room, I crazily begin to raise my legs. Picture an infant who just discovered she can kick her legs and wants to show-off her new skill.

Aaron responds in a sing-song way, "E-w-w-e -e, look at Miss Joan – she's ready to go!"

My brain is still like mush. I can't keep thoughts in my head long enough to complete a simple prayer. I begin to say, "Please Lord," but my thoughts vanish before I can finish my desperate plea for help. I hope God knows what's in my heart anyway.

Dr. M is not a Christian, but knows I am, and that I lean on my religious beliefs. During her morning rounds, she says with a smile, "I visited the Chapel today and said a prayer for you. I like to think we have the same God."

She places a Holy Medal on the wall above my bed, brushes my forehead, and makes her departure. I can't move my head to look at it, but I know what it represents – faith.

Later that evening, Carl and Donna sit at the foot of my bed. "The nutritional gunk they put up her feeding tube shouldn't be vanilla. It should be chocolate," Donna banters.

"That would snap her out of Zombieland," Carl sniggers.

Suddenly, my silence breaks. I chime into the goofy conversation, "Ya, you'd think they'd know better."

Did I just say that **out loud***?*

The words coming out of me sound odd though – as if I have mashed potatoes in my mouth.

But my God, I'm talking. After ten days of frustration and communicating by finger, I'm actually speaking!

I remember the Holy Medal on the wall, and request Carl take it down and hand it to me. Upon careful examination, the light-blue, silvery oval depicts the beautiful Blessed Mother as she rests on a cloud, her arms outstretched, as she welcomes me into her loving embrace. Beneath her is the printed word, "Medjugorje." I flip it over to look at the back. The upper left-hand corner reads, "Medjugorje Poruke" - Croatian for "Medjugorje Message." The lower right-hand side reads, "Mira Obracenja Molitva Posta," which means, "Peace, Conversion, Prayer, and Fasting."

Word spreads throughout the hospital about the miracle patient on the fourth floor. The woman who is able to speak after lying comatose for almost two weeks, and only after a Medjugorje Medal was given to her. Many curious strangers come to my room to witness the divine intervention for themselves.

I realize some may be hesitant to believe this is, in fact, a miracle. They might think the medal placed above my bed is coincidental, and there must be a medical explanation behind this. But I choose to think otherwise. I am indeed blessed. God has seen fit to perform yet another miracle.

I think about the Footprints plaque Terrie gave me. I have placed things in God's hands once again, and He has looked out for me. Even when I was too sick to ask for His help, He took care of me. During my solitary nights, when visiting hours are long over, and Carl has left for home, I am never alone. God has carried His precious child during these times of trial and suffering.

"If you stand before the power of hell and death is at your side, know that I am with you, through it all."
"Be Not Afraid" by Robert J. Dufford SJ

I no sooner thank the Lord, when I ask Him for help once again. My brain seems spastic, my body is racked with tremors. *Please Lord, make it stop. I can't handle this. It's driving me crazy!*

Each time I have an episode, I get a shot in my rear.

The feeding tube is now removed, but it's difficult for me to eat. I shake so horribly, it is close to *impossible* to drink. A cup of hot tea is out of the question.

I sob as I struggle to make a peanut butter & jelly sandwich atop my lunch tray. The packages are opened for me, but I fight with the slippery preserves which fall off my knife. All I can do is watch it wiggle.

Sandy, the private nurse, knows how much these tremors bother me. They make it difficult to fall asleep. She rubs my back until I drift off for a few short minutes. When I wake, I ask, "How long was I asleep *this* time?" I'm thrilled if it is for more than ten minutes.

She tries to distract me by talking about our children and of my going home and holding mine once again.

"Do you remember the pillow incident?" she reminisces.

I begin to laugh so hard, I can barely breathe. "Yes, that was hilarious. You should have seen your face. You went from serious, to laughter, to sheer horror."

~Chapter Four~

Another bone marrow aspiration is performed - maybe my fifth one - I lose count. It reveals that the potent ARA-C did the trick, crossed the brain barrier, and I am in complete remission. After three long months of hospitalization, on May 23rd, 1990, I am told I'll be going home tomorrow. This time I have no reservations, no fears of leaving the hospital. I am just *thrilled* to be going home!

Carl is ecstatic; his grin now a permanent fixture. We stop along the way at Burger King, my favorite fast food restaurant. Carl orders my usual – a Whopper, no pickle, no onion. I sob with frustration at not being able to hold the sandwich. Although the seat belt holds me in place, I barely manage to sit up, let alone eat the slippery monstrosity. Carl hands me napkin after napkin as he watches me clean the mess all over my face. He is just content to take me home.

Alice comes to live with us. She drives the thirty-five miles from Woodridge to Newark every Sunday evening and stays till Friday afternoon when Carl returns from work.

Unable to do most everything, I lie on the couch and watch TV. Alice takes over all the household chores. She cooks, cleans, does laundry, cares for the girls - and oh, babysits me.

I am like an infant and have to relearn everything - to reteach my brain to walk, talk, eat, and drink. I have to use a walker to stand; but I tell myself, *At least I am alive!*

Carl cuts my meat into tiny pieces. Unable to master drinking from a glass, I use a straw. What's next, a sippy cup? I choke at every meal. Even swallowing has to be relearned when the brain is injured. The mashed potatoes still seem to be in my mouth because I cannot speak clearly. My tender, peeled fingers cannot hold a piece of hot pizza. I get so aggravated. By the time it is cool enough for me to handle, it's too cold to enjoy. Carl cuts the hot pizza and I use a fork.

Every evening Carl helps me bathe. He lowers me into the tub and lathers the washcloth. I struggle to tend to myself. My lack of coordination makes this simple task difficult. He then washes my hair, pardon me - my head. It's insane we even use shampoo instead of soap. But at least we have the sense not to bother with conditioner.

I have a port in my chest for maintenance chemo, so he needs to clean it as well. It grosses me out when Carl carefully removes the dressing, rubs the Betadine-soaked swab around the dangling tube, and covers it with a clean bandage. This routine isn't painful, but it gives me the willies.

My joints and muscles have become stiff. I can't raise my arms above my head when Carl helps me into my pajamas. Come 10:00 at night, I'm so tired, but ache so much, it's difficult for me to fall asleep. It's painful to lie in our waterbed. I wish I had the potent drugs from the hospital to knock me out, but ask Carl to bring me some Tylenol instead.

I can't even manage to use the toilet on my own, but thoughts of going to a rehab center, and being away from home again is too much to bear. Carl offers to come home from work each day on his lunch break, although this entails a thirty minute drive each way, and he only gets a thirty minute break. I cross my fingers that I won't have to use the facilities until he returns. Carl is allowed to make up the lost time at the end of his day.

I've been prescribed so many pills, I can't keep track of when and how many to take. Carl lays them out each day. Steroids, chemo, anti-nausea, and on and on. One of them is methotrexate, a chemo pill taken three times a day at $28.00 each. Do the math. $84.00 a day times 30 days comes to a whopping $2,250.00 every single month. Can you say 'Visa'? It's no wonder the pharmacist questioned Carl's request to fill the entire month's supply all at once.

I also require a weekly methotrexate injection - the 'maintenance' portion of the treatment. Every other week, a blood draw is required to monitor for the cancers' return.

Our old, vinyl kitchen chairs with wheels come in handy. They allow me to zip around the kitchen with both hands free. I push off with my feet and roll from the microwave to the table to the refrigerator to the sink. I pull myself up and lean on the counter to wash a few dishes before my legs turn purple and give out from neuropathy. I can only stand for short periods before unbearable pins and needles, followed by numbing, force me to sit back down.

One morning, it occurs to me that my tremors have stopped. Alice brews a cup of hot tea which I enjoy for the first time in over a month. It's those little things we take for granted.

Despite the nurses' best efforts, drop-foot has become an issue as well. The muscles in my legs have shortened due to being bed-ridden. This causes me to walk on my tiptoes which adds to my imbalance. I consciously pull my foot down to the ground each time I take a step.

On weekends, Alice leaves for home, and Carl takes over full-time. Alice, God love her, cooks and freezes meals at home for her husband who is left to fend for himself in her absence. She catches up on her **own** laundry before returning to us. Our new lives are difficult, but we all adjust.

Two months after I've been home, I develop a horrible, gagging cough. The choking stops when I blow my nose.

"Theresa, can you get me a tissue?"

She walks over from the other side of the room.

"Theresa, I need another one."

She retrieves one again.

"Darn it, I need another one!"

The frustrated eleven-year-old has more sense than her mom and plops the entire box on my lap. Poor girl! I should be taking care of her.

I have a fever now, and I am instructed to return to the hospital. I break down and begin to shake as the hospital comes into view. *I'm so afraid I won't come home this time.*

I'm not admitted to Oncology on the fourth floor. I am taken to ICU, the Intensive Care Unit.

Later that day, Carl returns from lunch outside the hospital, and enters through the ER doors. Father Bob spots Carl.

"What are you doing here?" he asks.

Carl slams Fr. Bob into the wall.

"You call this is a freaking Catholic Hospital?" he shouts. "You've got a lot of nerve!"

"What's going on?" Fr. Bob asks in shock.

"Joanie's getting nasty phone calls while I'm at work from a 'Ms. Peters' at a collection agency. You people disgust me," Carl tells him.

"Whoa ... slow down ... take it easy! Tell me what has happened."

Carl explains we haven't even received a hospital bill. Whenever he contacts the hospital, he is told they are still compiling months of service and we should not worry. Yet, we've been turned over to collection.

"What?" Fr. Bob responds incredulously.

"Joanie gets worked up each time Ms. Peters calls. She calls Joanie a deadbeat. Joanie explains how she's unable to work, that she has to use a walker just to stand, for Christ's sake. Ms. Peters responds that she should get off her lazy butt and stuff envelopes if that's what it takes to pay this off."

It's not like we're irresponsible and have a debt from a glamorous cruise. We had no control over this. I believe it was Hillary Clinton who said every family is one diagnosis away from bankruptcy.

"Joanie actually said kindhearted Ms. Peters makes her feel like she shouldn't have fought so hard to stay alive and rack up this monstrous bill."

Stunned by this news, Fr. Bob apologizes. "I'm so sorry this happened. I'll get to the bottom of this. You two are going through enough, without having to deal with this."

Father Bob finds me in an oxygen tent. I cry on his shoulder once again. I am, of course, grateful for my life, but I know I've been short with the girls, and think I am being punished. "God gave me a second chance and I blew it!" No pun intended.

"God doesn't work that way," Father Bob reassures. Everything has changed in my life, and leaves me with a multitude of emotions - from profound gratitude to incapacitating aggravation and frustration. Things aren't moving as quickly as I think they should. Besides, the girls don't have a crystal ball to look into to predict what I want, when I want it, like I seem to expect.

A lung biopsy reveals double-pneumonia. Intravenous antibiotics are administered, breathing treatments begin, and once again, Father Bob anoints me with the Sacrament of the Sick.

The differences between my dad and I remain unresolved. Whenever I mention Dad's name, Carl cringes. Carl withholds my dad's actions until I drag it out of him. Carl has sheltered me from the truth until this point, aware of the importance of my maintaining a positive attitude. Carl knows the situation with my dad will hurt me, so he is hesitant to share the details of Dad's refusal to say his good-byes after the emergency surgery. I now understand the friction between the two of them.

I phone my father and beg him to patch things up with Carl. I fear dying and tell Dad I have thoughts of lying in a coffin, and of him and Carl not speaking to one another. Dad promises he'll take care of it, but he never does.

After several weeks of treatments, I return home to the couch.

Carl drives me to Aurora for my Tuesday chemo. He has to lift me into our tall Chevy Astro van. Chemo injections are $279.68. Carl wonders why they don't make it an even $280.00. He pays with a credit card. Dr. Madhavan sees this and chastises, "You shouldn't use a credit card for this."

"I have no choice," Carl says. "Our insurance doesn't cover out-patient visits; or Joanie's other medications."

"I had no idea!" responds Dr. M.

She turns to Allie, her receptionist, and says, "From now on, only accept the insurance covered portion."

Dr. M and I are like friends now, rather than doctor-patient. She introduces me as her daughter. Her of East Indian decent, and me from Irish roots, do not look anything alike. We get the oddest looks when she makes her introductions. Remember, she is only fourteen years older than I am, too.

She asks Carl, "Do you need money?"

Carl replies, "No," but she shoves a fifty dollar bill into his shirt pocket anyway.

I am expected for treatment every Tuesday morning at 11:00. After a period of time, I gain enough strength to get into the car without Carl having to shovel me in. Alice now takes me to chemo. With Natalie in tow, and the other girls back in school, we make the forty-five minute drive to the oncologist's.

Dr. M greets us at her office. Alice says to Dr. M, "Your receptionist tells me you don't charge *any* of your cancer patients for their co-payments. Who will take care of you in your old age?"

Dr. M points to the heavens above, and replies, "Gawd – Gawd will take care of me!"

Alice and Natalie stay in the reception area, as Dr. M whisks me into an empty room and leaves me to wait. She admonishes, "You shouldn't be out there with your low immune system. There are too many sick people out there!" When it is my turn, we move to a room set up with my chemo paraphernalia.

I cry on her shoulder when things are too difficult. She treats not only my body, but my soul as well. She is genuine in her care for the entire family and asks, "Is Carl eating? How are the girls coping with all this? What cute thing is Natalie up to?"

"Something is wrong with me. I think I'm going crazy, like Mom," I confide. "I either laugh like a hyena, or babble like an idiot. Once I begin to laugh, I can't stop. I even snort. Then my mood abruptly changes, and I bawl uncontrollably over nothing. It's embarrassing. I think I'm losing it. Sometimes I sit there with a Forrest Gump grin on my face, but this is one box of chocolates I'd rather not choose from."

"Trust me, if you were going to have a nervous breakdown, you'd have had one by now. The chemo has just heightened your emotions. It's temporary," Dr. M reassures me in a calm voice.

After my chemo treatments, Dr. M treats us to *Colonial Kitchen* for lunch. When the older girls have a day off from school, they join us. She gets a kick out of watching Theresa and Allison try to finish their large ice cream specials, aka, "The Kitchen Sink."

On most Tuesdays, however, it is just Natalie, Alice and me. After chemo, we go to Burger King and grab Natalie her 'Boo-ger King Crown', as Natalie so adorably points and begs. Tummies now full, we tackle grocery shopping. Alice pushes the shopping cart with Natalie's car seat in the front basket. At a snail's pace, I roll ahead in my wheelchair. I find it necessary to depend on it, rather than the walker. I ask Alice to retrieve items, as I cross them from my list.

Alice develops a departure routine. She places Natalie in her car seat, helps me inside, fastens my seat belt, and instructs the bag-boys to load the groceries on top of the wheelchair. She has a hatchback, and somehow they manage to make everything fit into that little car. If not for Alice's generosity, Carl would have to take Tuesdays off.

I get around slowly now, but I don't have free hands since they're wrapped around the walker, or "the clunker" as I call it. If things don't fit in my pockets, they are left behind. Alice fashions a brown canvas bag to hang from my walker. This makes life a little easier. I fill the bag with as much as it will hold - cordless phone, tissues, paper and pen....

I still need Alice to lug my portable, lighted, make-up mirror to the kitchen table on Tuesday mornings, as I carry the actual make-up in the walker bag. I struggle to apply cosmetics because I believe that between wig and make-up, I'll camouflage my illness.

Carl's sister, Harriet, again comes to the house for a few days to give Alice a break. We are very close, and I regard her as my own sister. She's an itty-bitty thing, but has the heart of a giant.

Words are not needed as we sit on the couch, hug each other tight, and cry. But our sobs turns to laughter as Natalie saves the somber moment with a little t-o-o-t! Out of the mouths (and other orifices) of babes.

Carl comes home from work one day, overwhelmed and exhausted. He snaps at the girls, "Your room is a pig sty, dirty laundry everywhere!"

Harriet disappears for a bit and returns wearing bright yellow Playtex rubber gloves, and holds a pair of salad tongs at arm's reach in front of her. A pair of Carl's dirty underwear dangles from the end. "You mean like these?"

A visiting occupational therapist observes my struggle to pick up the pennies she places on the table, and notes my tears.

She evaluates my sadness when I cannot lift Natalie to change her diaper, or manage the pull tabs.

She pulls Harriet aside, "Joanie seems depressed."

"Ya think?" Harriet responds. "Well, I guess since she has a terminal illness, and her entire world has been turned upside down – I think she has a *right* to be a little depressed!"

My taste buds are shot from the chemo, but for some reason I can still taste an apple. I can't manage the skin, so Harriet pleasurably peels one for me.

I am a whopping ninety-eight pounds. Dr. M tells me to eat anything I want to fatten myself up. Even candy bars. You don't hear a doctor say that very often.

I'm a cross between an alien and Frankenstein. I'm skin and bones; my glasses are too big for my thin face; I have a shiny, bald head; and the surgery on my jugular has left a huge, bright-red scar across my neck. It was not done with the utmost concern for cosmetics. It was done to save my life and close me up quick.

The two dimple-like scars on my chest from the failed ports, and the current dangling contraption I still possess, complete my ensemble. Thoughts of a 90's one-hit-wonder runs through my mind, *"I'm too sexy for my clothes, too sexy for my clothes, too sexy...."*

My sister, Ellie, uses a few of her vacation days to stay with us, to extend Alice's break. Ellie and I have always been able to talk. I bitch to her about everything that bothers me. I'm grateful for being alive, but at the same time, get so darn frustrated not being able to do the simplest things.

Every morning, Theresa fills a basin with water so I can wash my face and brush my teeth. I have to wait until evening when Carl is home for a full bath. I resent that everyone around me can walk from room to room, while I am stuck on the couch.

Our living room windows are broken and won't close. Someone needs to push them from the outside, while someone else cranks them in. It starts to pour one day. Little Allison can reach the kitchen window, and Ellie closes the bedrooms. But the living room windows still need attention. Theresa runs outside to push. I kneel on the inside, and try to help. I fall over as my knees sink into the couch. *I can't even close a damn window!*

When Ellie leaves, I find a note on my pillow. It's filled with encouragement. Ellie suggests I use the high standards I set for myself, to be a motivation, and not frustration. I sob as I think of her loving support and empathy, and about the many people God brings into my life to cheer me on.

When Alice returns, she stays for over six months, until I can care for myself.

One afternoon, the doorbell rings. Alice opens the door and one of the women from the group that questioned our "intentions" several months ago stands there. She smiles and hands Alice the cutest handmade bunny. It's gray, with little whiskers, and a tiny bow atop her head. It is attired in an adorable, calico-print dress.

"I made this for your daughter-in-law, in the hope she may find some comfort during her ordeal," she says.

I still have that little bunny. It continually reminds me of the kindness of so many, friends and strangers alike.

We eventually tell Alice it's okay for her to return home. She's given enough.

We are on our own. Carl sees the older girls off to school each day, and drops Natalie at the sitter's. Theresa becomes serious and is forced to grow up much too fast. She's always been mature for her age, but she has turned into a little adult. She helps her dad pack lunches in the morning, folds all the laundry after school, helps Carl prepare dinner, and changes Natalie's diapers.

Allison has been kept abreast of my illness from the beginning, but an eight year old only comprehends so much. She is given responsibilities as well, but somehow manages to pawn them off onto her big sister. She's still the care-free little girl who stares at her reflection in the TV screen as she smacks her gum and practices fly-girl moves.

Carl awakens one night in terrible pain. His description of the pain is all too familiar. It sounds identical to the appendicitis attack I had experienced years ago when I was in high school.

I am still unable to drive him to the hospital, and he is too stubborn to call an ambulance. So he gets on his bike and drives himself to the ER.

When the ER nurse peers at the motorcycle helmet lying beside him, she looks at him disgustedly and asks, "Do you know what we call these? **M u r d e r**-cycle helmets!"

"Congratulations," retorts Carl. "You went to med school for all those years to come up with that one!"

The nurse shoots him a dirty look and pulls the curtain shut.

While being examined by the doctor on call, Carl shares, "My wife thinks this is appendicitis."

"Oh, is she a doctor?" mocks the doctor.

"No," Carl replies, "but she did have hers removed."

A few choice words are exchanged before a prostate exam is performed. You have to wonder if *that* was medically necessary!

They decide to keep him overnight for observation. They say it's just gas. But he wakes in the middle of the night clutching his stomach in agony. The nurse tells him he needs an emergency appendectomy.

"Oh no, you've got to wait. My wife will **kill** me if she isn't here before the surgery," he gasps.

A neighbor watches the children so my sister Donna can drive me to the hospital. The entire event is so exhausting, instead of using the walker, when I arrive in the wee hours of the morning, I use my wheelchair. I see my physical therapist shake his head in disappointment at my use of the wheelchair. I become angry and think, *You have no clue.*

After the excruciating wait, the operating surgeon speaks to us after the procedure. "Good thing we operated in time. It was a mess in there; Carl's appendix had burst during the night," he says.

I begin to weep. I am gentle as I lay my head on Carl's arm, for *he* is the one in the bed this time. With everything we are going through, this is too much for me. I try to be the strong one, but I fail.

Carl is hospitalized for two weeks due to the severity of the surgery. Since I'm unable to be the caregiver, Carl has to fend for himself.

Once he gets the okay to get his incision wet, Carl and I wobble outside, and he fills our small kiddie-pool with water. He lowers himself into the two-foot above-ground oasis. Allison bounces along, and Theresa carries Natalie. She sets Natalie on Carl's lap.

I stay out of the sun due to the potent effects of the chemo. Dr. M has warned me about my sensitivity to the sun's harmful rays, so I sit a few feet back beneath a tree. Theresa helps me apply sunscreen profusely, and drapes a beach towel around me - even though it's ninety degrees outside.

I'm reminded how during the summer, my sisters and I made up games as we hopped over the colored cement patio in our back yard.

We danced around the kiddie pool, summoning the Indian rain gods.

"Minnie ha ha, Minnie skirts!" we chanted.

Natalie giggles as Carl bounces her on his lap. Allison shrieks when she is squirted with water. Carl then turns and squirts Theresa. She looks more perturbed than anything, at the childishness, dries herself off, and walks back into the house.

I warn Carl he should take it easy, but he continues the horseplay anyway. Like most men, he thinks he's the man of steel.

The next day, while in the shower, he discovers his entire left leg and groin are purple.

"Oh my God," I say. "You have to call the doctor!"

The doc tells him he has broken blood vessels and needs to take it easy, he is doing too much. *Imagine that.*

"Honey, I know we can't really afford it, but I think we need to hire someone to take over most of the housework. Look at Theresa, she's taking on the weight of the world; missing out on her childhood," I implore.

"I agree, we somehow *have* to come up with the money," Carl says.

And like an angel falling from the sky, we find a woman. If we provide the cleaning supplies, she'll do it for next to nothing.

"You girls still have to clean your bedroom, and help Dad around here, but we're hiring someone to clean **most** of the house." My gaze turns to Theresa. "We think you should have a break." A grin sweeps across her face.

The woman comes out once a week and I see a gradual change in Theresa. The cheerful little girl returns, and dances around the house singing, "Don't worry – be happy."

The cleaning lady is pretty much doing this out of the kindness of her heart, because after her gas expense, she only clears a few bucks.

A few months later, one of my bi-weekly blood draws shows lower than usual white counts. Dr. M recommends that I go to Rush Hospital in Chicago to obtain a consultation for a bone marrow transplant. The statistics of finding a sibling match are one in four. Terrie is pregnant, so she's out of the running. I am left with three possible chances. Thank God, sister Ellie is compatible and is a perfect match.

Carl, Ellie, and I take the long drive to the massive hospital complex in the city. The transplant team at Rush tells me I'm not strong enough to survive a transplant at this time. I am told my only option is to continue my maintenance chemotherapy.

One of my chemo visits doesn't go as planned. After I receive my injection, I complain to Dr. M that my stomach hurts. She retrieves a Dixie cup of Mylanta. As I tip my head back to drink it, she notices the appearance of hives on my neck. My chest begins to tighten. Her office is right across the street from the hospital, so she grabs my hand, we hop in her car, and head for the ER.

The ER nurse gives me an antihistamine injection, followed by an IV of the same. Dr. M says either I've developed an allergy to the actual chemo, or to the preservatives found in it.

The following week, chemo - without any preservatives - is administered inside the hospital as a precaution. This way, if a reaction occurs, I'll have the ER available. I hold my breath. Whoosh! Nothing happens. *So it is the preservatives.* From then on, I am given pure chemo.

While riding in the elevator to obtain my chemo one day, I overhear a woman discussing with another, how her mother is in a coma and doesn't know if she can hear her. I wish I had the articulation to tell her she most likely does! Continue to talk to her, and give her lots of encouragement. I heard *every* loving word when I was in mine.

Wally, my physical therapist, comes out to the house to teach me to walk with the walker, and regain some of my overall strength. I've graduated from using rolls of pennies in a pillowcase as weights, and need something heavier. Wally turns into the kitchen to search for a couple of soup cans.

I notice the girls cringe when he reaches into a kitchen cabinet without permission. What bugs my kids is that Wally feels just a little *too* comfortable in our house. He's invading their territory.

After several visits to the house, he stops ringing the doorbell and walks right in. Now it's on! It becomes a game to the girls. Theresa serves as lookout. She hops on the couch, looks out the window, and when she spots Wally pull into the driveway, she shouts to Allison, "Quick - lock the door!" The girls could have locked the door before his arrival, but this is more fun. He's *forced* to ring the doorbell.

One afternoon, when Carl is home, Wally barges into the house. Carl jumps from the couch and says, "You do know, we have a doorbell, right?"

"A lot of my clients cannot come to the door," Wally stumbles for an excuse, and walks past Carl.

He follows the "intruder" and says, "Well from now on, use it - that may prevent a bullet from ripping through your chest!"

Wally shoots him the same blank stare I've experienced a million times before. The lights are on, but evidently no one is home!

Poor Wally, he is a good PT, but has about as much personality as Lurch from the Addams Family. He's even built like Lurch - same awkward height, but broader, and with less hair. One day, he wants me to take a walk outside, but for the life of him, he's unable to grasp my need to wear my wig. I don't wear the hot and itchy thing in my own home, but feel naked without it in public.

After months of physical therapy, Wally explains how I need to trick my brain to walk without the walker. "Now I want you to walk while holding the walker up off the ground," he instructs. It's as though I need to command each step. Natalie objects, crawls behind, pulls at the walker, and shouts, "Down mommy, down!" It cracks me up.

I'll be damned if she walks before me, I think.

The animated classic, *Santa Claus is Comin' to Town*, pops into my head. *"Put one foot in front of the other and soon you'll be walking 'cross the floor. You put one foot in front of the other and soon you'll be walking out the door,"* I sing to myself.

I take both Wally's and Kris Kringle's advice to heart and it works. On July 16th, 1991, still too unsteady to walk outside, but in the safety of my own home, I take my first step without aid. (I know this exact date because I saved a calendar from that first year after my diagnosis.)

I progress steadily thereafter. I take short walks into town, holding onto Natalie's stroller for the balance I still need. Each day I go a little farther, until I'm able to walk the few short blocks to the post office. I am so thrilled at my recent progress, I telephone Alice at her home, and Carl at work, to tell them of my success.

I gain enough courage to walk without the aid of the walker. However, whenever I leave my home, or don't have a grocery cart or stroller to lean on, I use a cane. My wide gait prompts Dr. M to refer to me as 3-CPO from the *Star Wars* movies. Carl always holds my hand whenever we leave the house, and squeezes it tight each time I lose my balance.

I tell Carl my lack of balance affects me only when I stand now, so I *think* I can drive. I feel like I'm back in Driver's Ed as he nervously takes me out to the empty parking lot behind our house. I'm relieved and thrilled to discover I can drive safely once again. Thank God I have *some* normalcy back in my life.

Alice has come every Tuesday morning for over a year to drive me to my chemo. Now I can drive myself.

But when snow's on the ground, Carl takes me grocery shopping and to run errands. In addition to actually driving in it, I'm fearful of finding an unplowed parking lot I cannot walk through.

In October, Natalie's first birthday adds to our celebration of life. Dr. M comes over to the house, along with my entire family. We are all so excited that I am alive to see this day.

My dad says he has to work that day, so I explain to him that the party will be in full force when he gets off work, and he can stop by afterward. Sadly, he never comes. I make up excuses as usual on his behalf, but Carl and Dr. M grow disgusted.

In January, we receive an itemized hospital bill. Even though it was medically necessary, my private room is not being covered by insurance. Every item that came into my room was scanned. The shampoo bowl that was scanned when I had hair, never left the room. I was therefore being charged for *its* entire three months stay! The surgeries, ICU room, physical therapy treatments, and lab tests are all included. CAT scans, MRIs, and ultrasounds add to the total.

Who *knows* what the $14,000 in *"miscellaneous"* charges are. If it wasn't so sad, I'd find it laughable. Included with the huge paper stack are payment instructions. Our portion, after insurance, is a ludicrous $363,000!

"We Accept VISA and MasterCard" is stamped on the last page.

I'm sick to my stomach. I don't know what we are going to do. We send a payment each month, but this doesn't put a dent in the ridiculously huge bill. *We'll never be able to pay this off in our life time.*

Every payment we make prompts a telephone call. "We received your payment today, thank you, but when can we expect another? And could you double it?" Ms. Peters brazenly asks.

I try to keep this in perspective, and not let it get to me, but my heart drops every time the phone rings.

Dr. M asks why I'm depressed during chemo one week. Carl and I have decided to keep the financial hardship to ourselves, but I can no longer deal with this on my own. In desperation I blurt out my woes to her.

"Staying positive is crucial to your continued remission," she reminds me. She hugs me and says, "I'll talk to someone."

In the meantime, Carl visits the collection agency. He stands outside, a manila envelope in hand, asking each woman he sees, "Ms. Peters?"

"No," one answers.

"Ms. Peters?"

"No," says another.

"Ms. Peters?"

A woman walks past him, careful not to make eye contact, and heads for a car. She fumbles through her purse nervously searching for her keys.

"Ms. Peters?" Carl again asks.

"No," she replies.

"Of course you're not. We all know 'Ms. Peters' is a fictitious name, but now that I have your license plate number, I can find your *real one*. I'll find out where you live, your husband's name, even the school your children attend. I'll now make *your* life a living hell, and harass the shit out of *your family!*" he sneers.

Next month, Carl receives a phone call petitioning payment, but this time it's from a man. "We have been dealing with Ms. Peters," Carl snaps.

"Ms. Peters no longer works here," the man responds. "Now when can we expect another payment?"

The following week, Dr. M tells me about her recent conversation with the hospital administrator regarding the harassment. She delivered an ultimatum: She brings a lot of money in for the hospital. Either they make it right, or she walks. She *might* have also hinted at my possibly suing the hospital if the stress should bring me out of remission.

I receive a call from the hospital administrator. "I'm sorry for the unfortunate circumstances," he apologizes. "Because so much time had passed, the bill was routinely turned over for collection. As a sign of 'good faith', we will absorb the *entire* bill, and we have broken our contract with that collection agency. Had I been aware of the mistreatment of patients, I would *never* have dealt with these people."

Vindication at last!

The following spring, we have an eighth grade graduation party for Theresa. Dad says he has to work, but his wife, Elaine, will be there. My parents had divorced seven years earlier, and Elaine and my father were recently married.

Upon Elaine's arrival at the party, she apologizes for Dad's absence. I assume he will come later, and think nothing more about it. It isn't until Elaine is saying her goodbyes that I realize he had no intention of showing up.

Trembling, I mumble, "I guess this isn't important enough for Dad to want to come."

I do not intend to put Elaine in the middle of this mess. It must be difficult for her to be here, since she must be aware of the history Dad and I share. I've upset her, and she leaves the party.

Carl and Dr. M enter the kitchen to find me crying.

"He's not coming. He's really not coming!" I sob.

My father and I do not speak after that. He calls me on Christmas Eve to suggest we talk. I am relieved he wants to reconcile, but frustrated he has chosen tonight to do so. I am trying to get on with my life, and doing my best to enjoy the holidays. His unexpected call churns up disappointments deep inside me.

Several weeks later, he takes me to a restaurant for coffee and pie. It's difficult for me to articulate, and I don't want my words to be lost in tears, so I write them down. I include my feelings of being ignored, and of my children being ignored. I ask him why.

He reads the letter and appears nervous as he quickly devours his piece of pie. When he finishes reading it, he stares at me, but gives me no real explanation.

"Things will never be the same between us, but know I do love you," he finally says.

What the heck does that mean?

We drive home in silence. I am numb with confusion. Tensions have *always* existed between Dad and me. His way of dealing (or not dealing) with difficult or confrontational situations is impossible for me to comprehend.

When I was little, I idolized him. He was a strict, but loving father. I remember the tea party we had on the back porch.

I think of the time he showed me how to magically turn a lightening bug into a sparkling ring.

I recall how he struggled to carry the heavy TV from the living room into the kitchen, so we could watch *Family Classics with Frazier Thomas* while enjoying Sunday dinners. You *never* ate in the living room.

Dad was gentle when he removed splinters from my fingers, patched scraped knees, and helped with my sixth grade science project.

Things are different now. Something happened between my youth and adulthood. He seems cautious now, careful not to let me get too close. He has put up a wall between me, Carl, and his granddaughters.

I call him every Sunday. I tell him news about the girls, and about how I'm doing, in an attempt to draw him into conversation. I'm an open book. He responds, "Well, I should let you go. Nothing is new around here – just staying out of trouble." It's apparent I make him uncomfortable, and my calls are an inconvenience.

Clearly, my relationship with my father is complicated. Refused dinner invitations, and missed birthday parties and graduation celebrations over the past thirty-something years fester. I hit my head against the wall when my feelings are dismissed.

I pretend the problems don't exist, but when Dad and I have yet another disagreement, and I stop my Sunday phone calls, our communication ends.

When I realize our relationship is a one-way street, and my disappointment turns into anger, I decide it's best to end the charade. I wish I was a cold-hearted bitch though, because then this wouldn't tear me apart.

Regardless, I do love him – he's my Dad. As I struggle to understand his actions, I try not to be bitter. I won't lie, the hurt is still here, but I like to think I have forgiven him as God wants me to. I pray for peace in my heart.

" forgive us our trespasses, as we forgive those who trespass against us."

Many years ago, we had moved from our ranch house in Newark, to a beautiful two-story home in Lake Holiday, never taking into account what a challenge the stairs would prove to be.

I have to grip the railing when I go up or down. If things are small and lightweight, I rest them on my hip, and carry them, but if they are too heavy or too big, Carl does it for me.

I have progressed, but the burden still lies on Carl to get things done around the house. I try to clean as much of our home as I can, but he takes up the slack.

I lack the ability to change a simple light bulb (*How many Joans does it take...?*), and the strength to open a jar. The many things I can't do any longer falls into Carl's lap. I imagine the constant stress he must be under. Yet, he somehow manages to be *my* cheerleader, *my* rock.

Our marriage is a true partnership, as it should be. I lift his spirits when life is sometimes unfair; when he comes home from work exhausted, or when he's overwhelmed with all that needs to be done around here. I often think how God has made Carl for me, and me for him.

In addition to the appendectomy, Carl has both knees operated on due to the effects of his reckless childhood. He also requires surgery once on his left shoulder, and twice on his right. Each time wreaks havoc. I wish I could take care of Carl more. Neighbors shovel our driveway and mow our lawn. Everything else has to wait.

Normal protocol for "maintenance" chemo is eighteen months for children with this type of cancer – so they double it for me. After three long years of chemo injections and blood draws, I have my final treatment on the last Tuesday of April, 1993.

"I think we should celebrate!" Carl suggests.

"And invite all the doctors and nurses," I add.

Family and friends arrive to share in my victory. Of course, Dr. M attends, in addition to Dr. Zapata and his little boy. Carol, Leah, Sandy, and many of my nurses show up. It is a perfect day, as if the sun shines just for this wonderful jubilee.

As I look upon the many beaming faces that fill my yard, I hear the buzzing of stories of how they had been a part of my success. Life itself is a celebration. The many milestones I have accomplished are amazing as well.

Goosebumps surface and tears fill my eyes, as I watch a long line of people begin to form for the feast which Carl has prepared.

Carl takes my hand and leads me onto the deck which overlooks the gathering. My speech is garbled and weak as I speak into a microphone. My voice trembles as tears flow.

"Thank you all for coming, and for sharing this special day with us. I cherish **all** my family and friends. Each of you has been a part of this journey," I announce. Speech becomes more difficult as I choke back tears, but I continue. "Thank you Carl, for your love and support, I could never have done it without you."

I pause to regain my composure. "Thank you my beautiful, wonderful girls. I know things have been rough on you, to put it mildly. But most importantly, we've been fortunate to witness the Lord's many miracles. Who would have thought I'd be here talking to you today?"

I hand the microphone to my husband, who simply says, in typical Carl fashion, "Let's eat!"

JOAN AUBELE

~Chapter Five~

Fast forward to the year 2002.

Carl comes home from work and finds me wrapped in a bath towel, shivering at the top of the stairs.

"Watcha doing up there?" he says.

"Something strange happened to me while I was in the shower, and I was too afraid to walk down the stairs!" I mumble.

"What?" Carl exclaims.

"It was so scary – everything went dark," I say.

"Did you pass out?"

"No, but I couldn't see anything. Not a thing! I needed to reach for the wall so I wouldn't fall over. It was freaky," I continue. "Suddenly a pin-hole of light appeared and began to widen. But it was like looking through a kaleidoscope, and crumpled pieces of aluminum foil were coming at me."

"Oh honey, you should have called 911," Carl replies.

"I know. I wasn't thinking straight. Besides, I knew you were on your way home."

My speech is horrible and Carl says he's having a hard time understanding me.

"The kaleidoscope thing is gone, but now everything looks like it's in a children's pop-up book." I add.

Our insurance company mandates that I see the same neurologist I had seen when I was hospitalized a decade ago. Let's call him Dr. Quack, for all intents and purposes.

We visit Dr. Quack, and he flippantly determines that I suffer from an optical migraine, and sends me home. We leave his office confused. Okay, maybe an optical migraine would present similar symptoms temporarily, but *not* 24/7.

My symptoms persist, so Carl and I return to Dr. Quack's office. His diagnosis doesn't make sense to us.

"I told you, it is just an optical migraine," he says annoyed.

We further question his diagnosis, and he becomes irate. "Leave my office and never come back!" he shouts in broken English.

You've got to be kidding? I think. *He didn't really just say that, did he? What am I supposed to do now?*

I call the insurance company to explain how distraught I am and what has happened. They approve a consultation with a different neurologist.

I am sent to Dr. Wolfe who is amazing. He is sympathetic and listens to Carl and me tell our story for over an hour. He asks about my past neurological difficulties, and the current ones. Dr. Wolfe orders CT scans and MRIs to be done before our next visit.

When we next see him, Dr. Wolfe explains the MRI has revealed my brain is *riddled* with scars – new ones, along with old ones. "The radiologist reading the scan, questioned whether or not you were an alcoholic, there are so many affected areas," he tells us.

"What I believe happened to you ten years ago when you were in your 'zombie–state', as you call it, was that you had a stroke."

Well that explains a lot.

"I think a piece of fungus near your heart broke loose and traveled to your brain. I'm sure what you're experiencing is a TIA, a transient ischemic attack, or in other words - a mini-stroke. Let's get you on a low dose aspirin regimen, blood pressure medication, since it's a bit high, and cholesterol meds for good measure. We don't want this to happen again," Dr. Wolfe concludes.

Chemo does a number on a woman's cycle, so I've been taking low dose hormones to help regulate my crazy system. Chemo is supposed to jump start a woman into menopause, but lucky me; it has not.

Since Dr. Quack's original diagnosis was a brain irritation from the chemo, and not a stroke, I was never treated properly.

"And discontinue those damn hormones," Dr. Wolfe adds.

We leave his office in disbelief *and* relief, and head for the elevators.

"I can't believe it! I've had not one, but two strokes, and I'm barely even forty years old!" I wail.

I agree with Dr. Wolfe's assessment, but can't fathom that I've been betrayed by Dr. Quack for all these years. Carl wraps his arms around me as we travel down the elevator in silence.

After the initial shock, I eventually console myself. I should be grateful I have found Dr. Wolfe, and he's now taking care of me the correct way.

But, a stroke!

(One's chances of future strokes increase when you have had a previous one. My greatest fear is that someday I'll suffer a stroke so severe, it renders me unable to speak, and to express my love for those around me. I don't dwell on this, but realize the importance to say and do things for others right now.)

Mom passes away days before Christmas of 2003 from lung disease. She smoked for over forty years. I miss her so, but find comfort knowing that after twenty-six years of battling her inner demons, they have all left her. I find serenity that she is now at peace with the Lord.

Several months pass before I return to my usual wobbly self. The girls are growing up just like I dreamed, and I am happy to regain most of the duties of motherhood.

Natalie can't quite grasp why her mom isn't able to ride a bike like the other moms, catch a ball, or go for runs with her. She was born before she had the chance to know the mother who played baseball and tag with her children. She doesn't know about the mother who played guitar and loved to sing. I am the mother who takes naps to get through the day.

Over the years, I've been poked and prodded like nobody's business. I've endured multiple bone marrow aspirations, jugular surgery, and lung biopsies. I've undergone a liver biopsy, and surgery in both breasts, which thankfully proved to be non-cancerous. I've had hundreds of blood tests, numerous ultrasounds, and dozens of MRIs and CT scans.

I believe the fear of cancer's return will always be in the back of my mind. I confide in Carl, "I think I'd give up if it happens again."

He's confident as he replies, "No you wouldn't!" He knows me all too well. I'd be ticked, but I would fight like hell once again.

Carl and I own a 19' sailboat. We decide to take *Missadventures* out on beautiful Lake Delavan in Wisconsin for a nice, relaxing day.

When I first began sailing with Carl, I was scared to death, but I wanted to share in his new passion. I securely strapped myself into a life jacket, but still freaked out every time the boat heeled, even a little. My eyes grew big and looked to Carl for reassurance each time we rocked. His calm smile and firm countenance told me it was okay.

But a storm came out of nowhere, and I grew angry. As I hung on for dear life, I thought, I hate this! What am I doing here? This is **not** my idea of fun.

After a period of time though, something clicked inside me. I thought of the waves as a reminder I was alive. I no longer feared the storm, but welcomed it, as if to say, "Bring it on, I can handle anything that's thrown at me."

Even though almost twenty years have passed, the massive amounts of chemo have left me sensitive to the harmful rays of the sun. In fear of sunburn, I soak in the warmth beneath the shelter of the boat's canopy.

Sailing, for me, is now a peaceful time. I close my eyes, and feel the cool breeze as it blows through my hair. The gentle rocking of the boat soothes my soul as I reflect upon all of God's marvels. Carl cannot see the tears of joy, hidden behind my sunglasses, as I once again give thanks for my life.

"It'll soon be nightfall, we need to call it a day," Carl says as he snaps me out of my meditation. "It will take a while to get in."

"Aye-aye Captain!" I tease.

We tack back and forth as we head for shore, pull the boat out, and begin to break it down. It is dusk when Carl finally lowers the mast. I joyfully exercise my First Mate duties and gather bungee cords and ropes to secure it. I swat a mosquito from my face.

Another one lands on my arm. "These buggers are annoying!" I slap the back of my leg. One of the bites has turned into a giant welt. A swarm has formed around us.

"Quick - save yourself!" Carl jokes. He hurries me into the Jeep and slams the door. "I'll take care of the rest," he says.

Carl completes the task at hand in record time as he swats like a madman. He dives into the Jeep, like it's the getaway car in a robbery. He then locks the door for good measure.

"That was close," he says, swiping his forehead. "I barely got in with my life!" We laugh and head for home.

"I feel off," Carl complains the next morning. "Maybe I'm just tired from yesterday."

We have breakfast on the deck and spot our neighbor. We go over to talk to him, but Carl suddenly reaches for my hand and begins to sway. I almost fall over as he leans on me for support. *Me balance him?*

"We need to go in the house and call the doctor," I freak.

Our primary care physician tells us to come into his office right away. Upon evaluation, he rules out that Carl has suffered a stroke, but does suspect he is in the beginning stages of MS.

Muscular Sclerosis? I think. *My God, what are we going to do? If Carl ends up in a wheelchair, we'll just sell the house and buy a one-story, that's all. But I depend on **him** for so much. And if I'm unable to care for him as his disease progresses, who will? Goofy woman, take each problem as it comes!*

We see our neurologist. All the tests he has ordered have come back negative, other than the blood work which shows traces of West Nile Virus. He then refers Carl to an Infectious Disease Specialist.

The specialist is booked solid for several weeks, so he agrees to see us in the hospital's consultation room between appointments. By now, two weeks have passed, and Carl's symptoms still persist. "I'm not convinced this is indeed West Nile because you don't have the typical marks that are commonly found," the doctor says.

Carl explains that two weeks prior, he *did* have a strange lump on his arm, but it is now gone. The specialist dismisses our concerns, and recommends we go back to the neurologist. I refer to this as *"the medical merry-go-round."*

We return to the neurologist, who runs additional tests. He comes to the most bizarre conclusion: "The tests reveal there is no *recent* evidence of West Nile present, but there *were* traces in your system from the past."

Say what?

Months pass and the symptoms go away, but every once in a while, a mild version returns when Carl works a lot of overtime and is especially tired. His symptoms last no more than a few days, though.

The Lord always seems to look out for us. We're never sick at the same time, which allows us to care for one another. When one is down, the other is there to bring them up. Although Carl takes care of me most of the time, I do enjoy being able to reciprocate.

I've become sick again. I'm shedding weight. My clothes hang off of me. I am too weak to shop, or to care, for that matter. I am scared. I think this is the beginning of the end. I think my organs may be shutting down. Again I cry, and I pray. I look to Mom in heaven to give me the strength she had in her final days.

I'm not dying after all.

After numerous tests, the gastroenterologist discovers I have an intestinal condition called Microscopic Collagenous Colitis. This foreboding name refers to an inflammation of the colon that a health care provider can see only with the aid of a microscope. An increase in the number of lymphocytes, a type of white blood cell, can be seen in the layer of cells that lines the colon. An increase in the number of white blood cells is a sign of irritation. I am told the disease is not rare. What makes it rare in my case, is it's usually seen in people in their geriatric years.

"At one time or another you caught a virus of some sort, which in turn sparked your immune system to go into overdrive and attack your intestines. This in turn has formed scar tissue which affects your ability to absorb foods," the physician explains.

I find it rather ironic that twenty-four years ago I didn't have an immune system to speak of, and now I have too much. The condition is not life-threatening, just a pain in the butt, so to speak. I need to follow a rigid and strict diet in addition to the meds I must take three times a day to keep it under control.

No more chocolate, caffeine, carbonation, dairy, alcohol, seeds or nuts of any kind, or anything fried, spicy, or greasy, for this girl! My romance with food is now a thing of the past.

I told you every possible odd thing happens to me. Oh well, that's life! I went from a snug size 12 to a loose size 4. Although it keeps me thin, I would *not* recommend this weight loss program to anyone.

Ten years after the first TIA (mini-stroke), I have worked my way up to walking two miles a day. One day, dressed in my workout clothes for my morning walk, I bend down to retrieve a hair band which has fallen on the floor. Upon standing, I get a head rush, but it will not go away. A thick, black, squiggly line obscures my vision.

"I think it's happening again. I think I'm having another stroke. Get me an aspirin," I shout.

I'm already taking aspirin, but I think, *What the heck can it hurt?* Carl stumbles out of bed and digs through the medicine cabinet.

I give him a play-by-play account. After I swallow the aspirin, and a few minutes pass, I say, "It's the weirdest thing. I can see the black line moving to the left. Moving... moving... it's gone! I can see fine now. I think it's kind of silly to go to the ER."

"I think with your history of strokes, it would be stupid *not* to go," Carl replies.

We drive to the closest hospital, only to be told their MRI machine is not working or something. I am transported via ambulance to a larger facility.

I have suffered another TIA. I tell everyone three times' the charm. I've had my three, so now I'm through (although with my track record of suffering a stroke every decade, I'll be a little over sixty when I'm due for the next one. Gulp!). My speech has again worsened, and my handwriting is illegible. My balance is thrown off, and I am unable to manage stairs by myself.

The neurologist explains that a TIA leaves without damage, but since I've had a major stroke, and this being my second mini-stroke, my brain is traumatized.

An anticoagulant is added to my long list of meds. This new drug increases the seriousness of a potential fall, and I run the risk of bleeding to death like a stuck pig, as I so eloquently remind Carl.

Never a dull moment in the Aubele household!

Carl needs to work half shifts to care for me. He prepares all of our meals, and makes sure I'm set before he leaves me alone for a few short hours each day. He keeps up with the housework, along with playing cheerleader to me *again*.

I'm required to take short walks to regain my strength. Exhausted before I see the end of the block, I come home crying like a baby, saddened by the loss of my health once again.

"I'm so sick of this! For every step forward, I take two steps backward. How much is one person supposed to take?" I rage.

Carl listens to me cry and feel sorry for myself. He then gives me the pep talk I need. "I know it's not fair, hon, but you just have to do it."

He instructs me how to lift small hand weights to rebuild my lost arm strength. I allow myself another pity party. I feel so angry, so frustrated. I stay this way for several weeks. I then tell myself, enough is enough. Brush the dirt off and stop feeling sorry for myself. There are many people far worse off than me. What if I had suffered a full blown stroke again, this time never recovering? Having another set-back sucks (forgive me girls) but picking myself up again is something I'll just have to do.

Over time, I conquer the stairs. I hold the rail for balance, and climb slowly as I concentrate on each step. When I get too cocky, and move too fast, my foot catches the end of the stair and I clutch the railing tighter. *Thank you Lord for catching me again!*

My speech is intelligible in the mornings and after my naps, but when I'm tired, the mashed potatoes take over. However, it always makes for the *most* entertaining conversations when a person is hard of hearing. Between my muffled speech, and their deficit, it goes like this, "What? You said elephants play your piano?"

My biggest aggravation is my lack of articulation. Before I suffered the strokes, I was a corporate sales manager, orchestrating presentations to major companies. I spoke with the utmost confidence and grace. But now words seem to vanish from my mind as I struggle to relay the simplest of stories. Fortunately, as I fumble for words, my frustration apparent, I say to Carl, "You know what I mean." And he does!

At other times, the right words seem to flow. Weird.

If I write slowly, my handwriting is at best that of a third grader. My fingers seem to have a mind of their own; as they fly across the keyboard. Thank God for the backspace and delete buttons.

The memory loss is ridiculous. Sometimes I feel like Ray Raynor, the host of another classic Chicago children's show, who covered his jumpsuit with Post-It notes that held reminders of what to do next on the program (a cartoon, a commercial, a visit from Chelveston the Duck, etc.).

I have to write everything in my calendar. And I mean everything! Not just your usual appointment entries, either, but to return phone calls, balance the checkbook, or run to the grocery store. It's not like I forget where I am, or who my children are, just the routine chores of daily life. It's crazy, but I need to take notes whenever I make a phone call. Carl needs to "jump start" my memory, but eventually I recall events from the past. Whenever I lose my train of thought (which is quite frequent), I remind the girls that between my chemo brain, the strokes, and menopause, I'm lucky I remember my own name.

I'm back to card making, and I've started to create colorful woven scarves. I've worked my way back to walking two miles when I feel strong. Although my legs feel like rubber afterward, I have a great sense of satisfaction when I waddle over to the couch and plop down for a much needed nap.

It's strange. I can't stand for long periods of time, but I can go for fast-paced walks, or at least, what I call fast. It's as though the brisk pace tricks my brain, because when I slow down to enter my driveway, I look like I've had a few too many. Hey, what the heck, it gives the neighbors something to talk about.

I can't begin to tell you how important it is to get outside. It renews our spirit and keeps us in touch with nature. There's something about being surrounded with all of God's beauty, which creates the perfect setting for us to reflect, and appreciate one's life. We no longer see dishes piled up in the sink, or the overflowing laundry basket of unfolded clothes demanding our immediate attention.

I can now concentrate on what's *really* important. No matter how stressed or overwhelmed I may be, walks make these feelings disappear. Those of you who are able, go for that walk. I promise, the dishes and the clothes will *always* be there.

If you're confined to a wheelchair, sit outside and enjoy the beautiful sunshine. Years ago, when I was confined to a wheelchair, or needed to use a walker, I thrived sitting on the front porch. It did in the past, and does today, leave me with a sense of calm and purpose.

One morning, while enjoying my deck, I begin to cry. I feel God's presence so intensely. I feel Him in the breeze rustling through the trees as I bask in the grand sunshine. It is kind of like God saying, "Remember, I'm sitting here with you."

Carl gives me the support and determination I need to get through it all. He has always shown me the true meaning of the marriage vows we took when we were just seventeen and eighteen years old. *"In sickness and in health."* I don't think he really knew what he was in for though.

We are crazy in love, and strive to make one another happy. It's now just a part of our lives. It's the little things, along with the big. He's gifted with a crazy sense of humor (which I adore), and without fail, he pats me on the behind each time he walks by me as I stand at the kitchen sink. After every dinner, he leans over, kisses me, and says, "Thanks for dinner, honey."

When he comes home from work, I stop whatever I'm doing to greet him. I realize this sounds very 1950s like, but I'm just so happy to see him. (I promise, I do not greet him dressed in pearls and heels bearing his pipe and slippers like June Cleaver did.)

Each night, as we fall asleep, we make sure we are touching – even if it's just our fingertips or toes. It reminds us we're present for one another. I try to do as much as I can for him, for he knows I love him with my entire heart, mind, body, and soul.

I think that's what God wants, for all of us to love with our entire being. In a perfect world, if we all lived for one another, there would be no violence of any kind, no hatred, and no wars.

~Chapter Six~

I begin to have unexplained pains. I am scheduled to have a procedure done. The procedure is not life-threatening, but I am certain something serious will be found. I feel an urgency to complete my book once and for all. I feel the same clear message I have experienced from the Holy Spirit many times before. But this time I think He is trying to tell me I am going to die soon, so if I am going to share this story with others, I had better do so quickly.

I confide in Allison, "I'm afraid they'll discover something horrible again, and it's time for me to die."

"Mom, you shouldn't think you're going to die, but rather God is reminding you to finish your story," she says with comfort in her voice.

But my prayers have been answered. I'm fortunate to have been a part of my girls' growing up. I was around to sit at the kitchen table and talk about the drama at school, or about the cute boy in their class. I held them as they cried, when life didn't seem quite fair.

I was there when they went on their first date, saw them off to prom, away to college, to become the confident, young women they are now.

Theresa donates countless hours to her church's youth ministry program. She's been to Puerto Rico on several occasions to do mission work. I'm happy to say she's no longer that serious little girl taking on the weight of the world. She's cheerful and witty, but takes her responsibility for others' well-being to heart. She volunteers at a food pantry, and her empathy shines through.

Allison has found a wonderful man to share her life with, and they recently celebrated their eight year wedding anniversary. She has just graduated nursing school with honors, and anticipates a fulfilling career helping others. I have no doubt she'll be an awesome caregiver! Her freckles have vanished, but her blue eyes still melt my heart. The cycle of life continues. Carl and I have been blessed with two adorable grandsons.

Natalie, the youngest, is the "adventurer" of the three girls. She flew to a ski resort in Breckenridge, Colorado for what was supposed to be a temporary job. She loved it out there, and then planted her roots. She now has a baby of her own! She also has a huge heart and is a wonderful mother. She's started a mom's group in her hometown, organizing events for two-hundred and thirteen women.

All three have a bit of smart-ass in them, just like their Dad. I adore that they're clever and quick. I'm proud of each of them, and make a point to tell them often.

My children, having children, is monumental for me. At one time I was concerned about not being alive to raise my own children, and here I am, blessed to be here for theirs!

That Carl and I were so innocent, and began our family together at such a young age, unaware of what our future would hold, fills my eyes with tears. I often think how difficult it must have been for him. I've often said it was harder on Carl than it was on me. It must have been terrible as he faced the probability he'd have to say goodbye. My big, strong husband was powerless, his future uncertain. He not only went through my many medical roller coaster rides, but continues to reassure me I can succeed in anything I want to do, such as write this story.

After all we've been through, we've learned to never skip an opportunity to say, "I love you," and to always share what each of us means to one another. We never know if this will be the last time we may get to utter these words. Don't get me wrong, we do argue, but we are quick to kiss and make up. We realize life is too short, and shouldn't be wasted on the trivial.

We take a vacation to beautiful Puerto Rico. My favorite part of the trip is when we hike through steep (at least for me) paths in the Rain Forest.

I tire, so Carl leaves me at a rest area while he surveys the trail ahead. As I take in this breathless site, I realize the relevance in this. I had held onto Carl's hand tightly, followed his every step, and counted on him to safely see me through. I had done this so many times before when I put my trust in the Lord. It reminds me He has always been there for me. I again feel a great sense of calm mixed with gratitude. I have been bestowed with not one, but two rocks upon which to build my castle.

I get frustrated with life's unfair difficulties, but then someone comes along and says, or does, the right thing. They put me back on track.

People don't always handle situations the way we'd like them to. The neighbor I considered a friend must have found my travails too difficult to bear and ignored me. But the neighbor who wasn't a close friend, rose to the occasion, and cared for the girls on weekends, and found time to take Theresa and Allison to shop for school supplies and their new fall wardrobes.

It's fortunate the good outweighs the bad in this world. I've shared some of these details to demonstrate how vital our treatment toward one another is. We never know how what we say or do, or don't say or do, impacts someone else's life; *for good or for bad.*

We need to take responsibility for our actions. If we screw up, as we all do, we need to be accountable. This is so lacking in today's world. Tell the wronged person you're sorry, and most importantly – learn from it.

Better yet, stop and think about what you are about to say or do. Is it something you would want done to you? Something that would hurt if it were said to you? If we thought about this more, we wouldn't have half the problems in this world.

Life is too short to dwell on negative things that are not in our control. We do possess the power to live our lives with great intensity, love, and purpose.

Sometimes we need to walk away from those who wrong us, and cherish the ones who are good to us.

For every negative that comes our way, many more positives appear to offset them. For instance, when I was pregnant with Allison, before I became ill, Carl's dad, John, was concerned about me going downstairs, leaving the new baby alone in the apartment while I did laundry. He purchased an apartment size washer and drier for me. When we moved to Newark, John bought us full size units when these conked out.

Many days, after his long shifts at work, John swung by the hospital in his dark blue coveralls to see me. I remember one time in particular, when I was in my zombie-state, I leaned over to hug him and wouldn't let go - I was so grateful. He had to pry my arms from his waist when he needed to leave.

Years later, Carl and I invited his parents over for a nice dinner, but when Carl was required to work late, the three of us enjoyed the meal. At the end of my evening with Alice and John, I blew out a candle in my living room which spilled red wax on my white carpet.

Carl's father (he was about seventy at the time) got on his hands and knees to help clean up the mess. That simple gesture displayed great respect from him. There were times in the past when we'd butt heads, to be sure, but at the end of his life I had great respect, love, and admiration for him.

The more I follow the Holy Spirit's direction to proceed with this story, and the more I do for others, the stronger and happier I feel. I wake each morning flooded with memories of things to be included in this book, and jot them down before I forget them. It's as though He's saying, "and don't forget this!"

"If today you hear His voice, harden not your hearts." Psalm 95

It's been suggested by many people that I write this story. I believe it to be the Holy Spirit at work through them. I have attempted to complete this manuscript for over twenty-five years, but my frequent ill-health, computer crashes (causing me to lose the entire story – twice!), and my poor typing skills, due to the strokes I've suffered, have placed almost insurmountable obstacles in my way.

The original intent to put this story on paper was as a form of therapy. But I now feel the desire to share my discoveries with others, in hopes they too will be inspired to live their lives to the fullest.

A friend from my prayer group told me about a ninety-eight year old woman who was asked the secret to her longevity. "Each morning, I say, 'Thank you Lord for this day. What can I do for someone else today?'" she modestly replied.

This sums up everything I have learned. We should live our lives doing for others. I begin my day with the sign of the cross, if nothing else, and plan to do good for someone.

I'm by no means trying to pawn myself off as an accomplished author. My thesaurus is my new best friend as I search for the words that best describe my feelings in this book. I do believe it would be selfish on my part to have been given all these opportunities at life and to do nothing with them. I feel I *must* share my amazing experiences with others, and all I've learned along the journey.

I'm simply a wife and mother who now has a deep appreciation for her life. I imagine most people come to this same conclusion after they have lived a long and fruitful life. But, we never know when our lives will end - it may be sooner than we'd expect (quite possibly at twenty-nine).

Ask any terminal patient. They know. Time has slipped away, catching them off-guard. Let's face it folks, no one wakes up in the morning knowing this will be their last day on earth; prepared, satisfied, that we've done and said everything we wanted to. We sometimes skate through life, not taking our full responsibility for others seriously. I've been blessed with a second chance to realize this, and a third, and a fourth....

I don't know what the future holds for me, but I do know this - I'm going to make every moment count, and love like there's no tomorrow! I've stared death in the face countless times and was fortunate enough to be on the receiving end of some pretty amazing miracles. I want to leave a legacy for my children, one of faith, love, endurance, and compassion.

I am living proof that miracles aren't a thing of the past, and they don't solely appear in history books. They are all around us - today, and every day.

We can find God everywhere. Look for Him in that gentle breeze rustling through the trees, in a breathtaking sunset, a child's laughter, in a loved one's touch, or in a spouse's love and commitment for one another. We can find Him in a stranger's smile, in a friend's generous compassion, in our mother's whispers of encouragement.

One of my favorite parts of the Mass is when I watch the different types of reverent people walk down the aisle after they receive Holy Communion. Some old, some young – while some bounce along, others struggle to walk. I am reminded God has now entered each heart. They are the living, breathing Disciples of Christ. Each person has been given a gift – the choice to pass this love on to one another.

"I believe, I believe, I shall see the goodness of the Lord in the land, in the land of the living." Responsorial Psalm

I feel a bond, a kinship if you will, when we join hands and recite *The Lord's Prayer*. Take the time to reflect on each sentence. Resist the urge to ramble through the memorized words most of us have said since we were children.

I'm no Mother Theresa. I become angry if someone wrongs me. Heck, I still struggle with the issues with my father! But despite my faults, God has taken me under his wing.

Please understand we are *all* capable of receiving miracles in our lives. We just have to open ourselves to the reality of God's love, and to gracefully accept his many blessings.

I cannot stress the importance of reaching inside yourself to find your spirituality. That is why we are here in the first place! We need to live as God wants us to. He wants us to be happy, to care for and to love one another, and to make a difference in someone's life.

Yes, look to God when you are in need of help, but more importantly, thank Him for all the good in your life. If you ask for His help to work through any difficulties you may experience, you'll discover you have the strength to do the unthinkable.

Whenever I'm confronted with a conflict, and cannot resolve it on my own, I look to God for the answer. I pray, asking Him for direction. I either discover the solution to my problem, or decide it best to let it go and make peace with it. There's no reason we have to endure anything on our own, we just need to ask for His help.

Make your life count. Go that extra mile for a friend in need of your time; wake up each morning like that wise ninety-eight year old woman, anticipating how we can better help someone today, and to make this a better day than yesterday.

I've been blessed with the opportunity to share my story with several area churches. I was honored to be the keynote speaker at an "American Cancer Society's Relay for Life" event, in the spring of 2013.

I still keep in contact with Carol, Leah, and Sandy - my angelic nurses during the cancer hell journey. Carol, Sandy, and family, were present when I delivered my most recent speech during a cancer survivors' picnic on "Cancer Survivors' Day" in June, 2014.

I'm in no way trying to 'toot my own horn' as Mom used to say, but I now *think* I've found my purpose. I pray God lets me continue to share His marvelous wonders with many for years to come.

My hope is to inspire *anyone* going through a rough patch in their lives – be it physical, financial, marital; or whatever crisis finds you in despair.

I've summarized all that I've learned throughout my crazy life into a simple twelve-step program for you to live your life *without regret.*

Many of these suggestions are directed toward people who are going through a cancer journey, but I believe they can be used for *every* trial and tribulation we encounter throughout our lifetime.

1. **Never capitalize the word cancer.** This gives it too much authority and power! Remember, you have cancer - cancer does NOT have you.

2. **Kick-start your relationship with God.** Pray more than you ever did before. Ask Him for help, to be sure, but also thank Him for every little accomplishment. You're never alone if you embrace that Christ's love is always with you. I believe when I was delirious with fever or when I was in my "zombie state," I was actually being carried by the Lord - such as in the "Footprints" poem.

3. **Find pleasure in the smallest of everyday things.** Focus on all the things you *can* do, not on what you cannot. Celebrate every victory and milestone throughout your life.

4. **Laugh.** Laugh till your side hurts! Surround yourself with people that do. It's compatible with every drug, and there are no side effects whatsoever!

5. **Never miss an opportunity to say I love you.** Always let those around you know how special they are to you. Don't be afraid to say you're sorry if you've wronged someone, but don't beat yourself up about it; just do better next time.

6. **Find your passion.** It could be in raising your children or to simply cherish your grandchildren. Maybe you've dabbled in painting or creative writing. Go for it. Now's the time to explore these once again. A friend of mine found her passion in gardening. The sky's the limit people. Make those vacation plans, set those goals, and look to the future.

7. **Go for walks whenever you can.** Get outside even if you're being pushed in a wheelchair. I do most of my thinking and spiritual healing when I do! Learn to appreciate the beautiful nature around you and God's many magnificent gifts.

8. **Live your life for one another.** It's that simple. Spend your time doing for others. Be kind, be compassionate, be fully present! Be an inspiration to someone.

9. **It's okay to feel sorry for yourself.** Give yourself permission to grieve over the loss of your health. Even wallow in self-pity for a day or two. But after that, pick yourself up, brush yourself off, and kick butt once again!

10. **Get yourself a proverbial cheerleader.** A good support system is so important. They can pick your spirits up if you're still bummed after the allotted two day grace period. Heck, people who try to lose weight have a friend to coach them on, and so should you!

11. **Don't be afraid to lean on someone.** It's not a sign of weakness. The strongest people are the ones who ask for help. It keeps us human and makes us humble. You'll find that people want to help. I urge you to join a cancer support group. Everyone there is either going through or has gone through the same thing. They may shed some light on the difficulties you are experiencing as well as alleviate some of your fears.

12. **Fight.** FIGHT LIKE HELL! No matter what your prognosis, no matter how bleak the situation may seem – FIGHT. Because with God in your corner, you will create your own success stories!

My wish for you today is that it doesn't take total devastation in your life, as it did me, to appreciate the wonderful miracle of our very existence. To appreciate every day as if this may be our last. To never miss an opportunity to say I love you, to find grace in our lives *no matter* what struggles we are enduring, and to simply ... *relish the dance!*

Carl and Joan at their wedding reception, Saturday, May 6th, 1978

~Acknowledgments~

A heartfelt thank you to my daughters Theresa, Allison, and Natalie for giving me the determination to fight in the first place. Thank you for handling your less than perfect childhoods so well. The laughter and tears we shed have created the most caring, loving women. I'm so proud of each of you!

I'm so thankful for my mother-in-law, Alice, and your overwhelming unselfishness. You saved an entire family; and we are forever grateful. Your life is an inspiration, as you share joy with everyone who has the pleasure of meeting you. I'm forever grateful to you for raising the son you did.

Thank you to my sisters Terrie, Ellie, Donna, and Harriet, for helping Carl run the household in my absence, and to my dear friends Tammy and Edna for helping out on weekends with the children, thereby saving Carl's sanity! We don't know what we would have done without any of you.

A special thank you goes to Dr. Chitra Madhavan for recognizing the need to treat my physical being, and my spiritual one as well; for realizing that we both pray to the same God; and who acted as an instrument of God's intentions. I recently contacted Dr. M to ask her permission to include her photograph in this book. The letter I received from her was so heartwarming, I wish to share it here.

"Dear Joan, Your letter brought me to tears. I was wondering what happened to you when I didn't get a Christmas message. Now I am okay, knowing all is well with you. Your struggles should be an inspiration to all. I think of you often. I always think that the reason I was put on earth was to be involved in your care. Definitely God's guiding hands were the real gift for us all. Rather than me getting any credit, it was my teachers in NJ who taught me, that should get it. My teachers were Dr. Arnold Rubin MD, Dr. Arthur Spielnogel MD, and Dr. Barry Fernbach MD. Without them I couldn't have done what I did. You take care. Say hi to all, especially Alice. ~ Chitra"

Thank you to the wonderful nurses and all involved in my care at Mercy Center. A special thanks to Carol, Leah and Sandy. I now know you are angels in disguise. You treated me with utmost dignity and respect in my darkest of times.

God bless Father Bob, your comforting words helped me through the most difficult time in my life.

A special thanks to my beloved mother, who affectionately called me her little rosebud. She gave me a strong religious foundation, and taught me the importance of prayer. She taught me how to look to God, and by her example, how to be a strong woman, enabling me to triumph over my many struggles.

A huge thank you to Mary Ellen Aschenbrenner and Stephen Dunn from the Somonauk Public Library Writers Group. Published writers themselves, they assisted in the composing of this story – more angels brought into my life.

Thank you to Father Don DeSalvo for answering my many questions about the history of the "Medjugorje Medal."

Thanks to the many; Aunt Pat, Aunt Marge, Marie, my sister Ellie, Carl, my children, Mary Ellen and Stephen who encouraged me to write this. I believe the Holy Spirit was working through all of you.

Most importantly, all thanks to the Lord. I'm grateful for not only letting me live, but to have been given the many opportunities to realize life's important lessons throughout my dance. I dance for you!

"Dance then wherever you may be; I am the Lord of the Dance, said he, I'll lead you all, wherever you may be, I will lead you all in the Dance, said he."

JOAN AUBELE

~Resources~

If you or a loved one has been diagnosed with cancer, I recommend you visit the American Cancer Society's website at: www.cancer.org

The site is packed with information. There is a cancer glossary, so you will understand the terms you will hear at your doctor visits. The site includes information about arranging transportation to and from chemo and radiation therapy if you are unable to do so on your own; numerous support groups to help you cope; suggested ways to stay healthy; and even beauty tips to use during treatments. Don't neglect to reach out, help is just a click or a phone call away.

In addition to reaching out to your local church for spiritual assistance, you can contact Catholic Charities at:
www.catholiccharitiesusa.org

Joan Aubele was born and raised in Chicago, and now resides in rural Lake Holiday – Somonauk, Illinois - with her husband. They've raised three daughters, and to date, have three little grandsons. Several years ago, her oldest daughter treated her to a weekend, inspirational, Christian women's conference. Although spending time with her family remains her number one priority, she dreams of someday being one of those speakers – to help make a difference in people's lives. She currently sells scarves of her own design to inspire women, and donates a portion of the proceeds to the American Cancer Society.

Joan loves hearing if, and how, her story has moved you. She can be reached at: P.O. Box 653 Somonauk, IL 60552, or at: jathedance@yahoo.com

CPSIA information can be obtained
at www.ICGtesting.com
Printed in the USA
LVOW04s1618180316

479779LV00018B/744/P